Economics
and the Family

Economics and the Family

Edited by
Stephen J. Bahr
Brigham Young University

LexingtonBooks
D.C. Heath and Company
Lexington, Massachusetts
Toronto

Library of Congress Cataloging in Publication Data

Family Research Conference, 8th, Brigham Young University, 1979.
    Economics and the family.

    Sponsored by the Family and Demographic Research Institute of Brigham
Young University.
    1. Family—Economic aspects—United States—Congresses. 2. Family
policy—United States—Congresses. I. Bahr, Stephen J. II. Brigham Young
University, Provo, Utah. Family and Demographic Research Institute.
III. Title.
HQ728.F324   1979   306.8'0973   79-47985
ISBN 0-669-03623-4

Published simultaneously in Canada.

Printed in the United States of America.

International Standard Book Number: 0-669-03623-4

Library of Congress Catalog Card Number: 79-47985

Contents

List of Figures

List of Tables

Preface

The high inflation rate in recent years has heightened interest in economic problems. Almost everyone is concerned about the shrinking dollar and how it affects individuals and families. There is a need for increased study in this area, particularly of the economic roles of females. To help fill this need, the Family and Demographic Research Institute of Brigham Young University chose economics and the family as the theme of its eighth annual family-research conference. The purpose of the conference was to bring together scholars from a variety of disciplines to assess the state of the field, promote interdisciplinary cooperation, and stimulate needed research. This book of selected conference papers was planned to help fulfill these objectives and to serve as a resource and catalyst for further work in family economics.

Chapter 1 introduces the reader to the study of family economics. In it Gordon Bivens identifies various ways in which the family is an economic entity. Particularly valuable is his discussion of nonmarket activities and their economic impacts. He concludes with an agenda of needed research.

Part I includes three chapters on the economic roles of wives. In chapter 2, R.K. Armey examines the economic value of housework and concludes that in terms of *real* income, housewives are paid for their services. Economic loss occurs when a housewife loses her "employment" through divorce. This chapter is a provocative one that is likely to stimulate debate and research in this area.

One common economic role for the wife is to enter the paid labor force. In chapter 3 Chadwick and Chappell have analyzed trends and effects of female employment. They found that increases in female employment over the past fifty years have been largely in the middle class. In their sample a wife's employment has had little effect on life satisfaction or basic spending patterns.

Domestic garment-making is one activity that wives and other family members sometimes undertake in an attempt to reduce clothing costs. Contrary to popular belief, this practice is economically inefficient according to the analysis of Robert Steadman in chapter 4. He recommends the purchase of used garments (through garage sales, charity stores, and second-hand stores) as an alternative.

Part II of this book contains two informative analyses of fertility. Hyman Joseph reports in chapter 5 that fertility tends to be higher when the husband's income is moderate rather than low or high. The wife's income has a negative relationship with fertility, and this relationship is stronger at intermediate than at high or low income levels.

In chapter 6 Lawrence Carter concludes that economic factors have their greatest effect on the birth of the second child. Apparently, social factors constrain economic influences on fertility at other birth orders. Consistent with other research, Carter found that the husband's income is positively related to fertility and the wife's income is negatively related to fertility.

The effects of various public policies on the family have been frequently debated among policymakers and scholars. The final section of the book includes four timely chapters on this topic.

Chapter 7 is a skillful review and synthesis by John Bishop of income-maintenance studies. The data reveal that when welfare payments are expanded to provide benefits for two-parent families, marital dissolution rates increase. This is the opposite of what policymakers and students of welfare policy expected. Bishop's interpretation of these findings provides new insights into the way economic variables affect family life. He concludes with some useful suggestions for public policy and future research.

Chapter 8 is an evaluation by Jacqueline Kasun of a public policy directed toward reducing adolescent pregnancy. She observes that the problem of teenage pregnancy has been exaggerated and that the facts do not justify governmental regulation of fertility. Her findings are not consistent with prevailing opinions about adolescent pregnancy and raise questions about public policy in this area.

A program to increase the economic self-sufficiency of teenage mothers is presented and evaluated by Schinke, Gilchrist, and Smith in chapter 9. They found that the program participants showed improvement in several skills necessary to obtain employment. Their findings will be useful to those involved in programs to reduce unemployment.

In the final chapter Yung-Ping Chen examines how changes in the structure of American families have affected the popularity of the social-security system. He notes that the growing numbers of never-married, separated, and divorced persons may be dissatisfied with social security because benefits are less for single than married persons.

It is apparent from the research in this volume that contemporary wisdom is not necessarily reliable. The data in several of the chapters contradict accepted "facts." For example, the welfare system in the United States has been criticized severely because single-parent families receive larger benefits than two-parent families. According to critics, this provides an economic incentive for marital dissolution. However, as reported by John Bishop in chapter 7, when welfare payments were made available to two-parent families, the rate of marital dissolution increased rather than decreased. The prediction of experts was just the opposite of what actually happened.

Another recent example is the California Family Law Act of 1970, which mandated equal division of marital assets and debts in divorce. Many supported this law because they felt it would help females obtain a more equitable financial settlement. A recent analysis by Seal[1] indicates that financial settlements for females under the new law have actually been worse than they were under the old law.

These two examples show that common sense and expert opinion are not sufficient. Systematic analyses of the economic consequences of proposed and existing policies on families are needed. A challenge for scholars is to extend the work of this volume and begin conducting these much-needed policy analyses.

I thank the participants of the conference for their contributions. Ruth Barlow, Kristen Goodman, and Howard Bahr were particularly helpful in organizing the conference and in the preparation of this manuscript. Yung-Ping Chen made some useful editorial suggestions. The Family and Demographic Research Institute of Brigham Young University provided financial support.

Note

1. Karen Seal, "A Decade of No-fault Divorce: What It Has Meant Financially for Women in California," *Family Advocate* 1 (no. 4) (1979):10-15.

1 The Family as an Economic Entity: Some Evolving Observations

Gordon E. Bivens

Any society must have a system by which the economic claims of each of its members are determined. These claims are the individuals' sources of livelihood. Kyrk has identified three types of claims present in our society:

1. Contract claims: those claims established through market transactions (wages, dividends, interest, and so on).
2. Statute claims: those claims established by law (old-age benefits, public education, and so on).
3. Family claims: those claims established by familial support systems (that is, who you are).[1]

It is through the third type of claims that the family is seen as of major significance since probably half or more of our population today obtain a major portion of their livelihood through economic claims on the family.

For purposes of this discussion, a *family* may be defined as "a group of interacting individuals, most often related, who have mutual rights and responsibilities." Obviously, this definition is not finely honed, in fact, not even tightly drawn, but it will serve the present purposes.

Also *economics* is understood as the administration of scarce resources. This broad conception of economics allows for the inclusion of the development, maintenance or conservation, and allocation of scarce resources among competing uses or ends.

Families and the Larger Society

The interdependence of the family as an economic entity and other large segments of society may be viewed as shown in figure 1-1. From this familiar circular diagram, it is clear that the households—the bulk of those being families—are significant elements in the broad economic sense. They obviously are consumers of goods and services provided through both private and public means. But, in addition, households are providers of many important factors of production to firms and public agencies; therefore they are important in an economic sense in that way too. Families as consumers *and* producers will be important foci in this discussion.

1

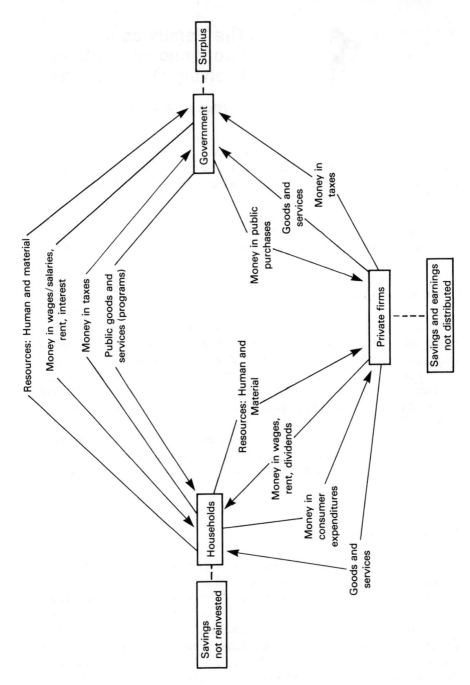

Figure 1-1. Interdependence of Households, Firms, and Government

Families as Producers

The decline of the family as a producing unit in society is often heard. However, I suggest that debating its decline obscures a larger point. What is important is that the output of families has changed, or rather that the relative importance of its different outputs has changed. At an earlier point in history, families' efforts resulted in easily identified, saleable products—milk, butter, eggs, textiles, shoes, café meals, and so on; today the output of families is less tangible, and we may be less ready to talk about the marketplace aspects of that product.

Family Output: Human Resources

Contrary to the popular notion that families are not producing units, I would maintain that families today continue to be important in a productive sense. One of the main outputs is human resources. I am *not* suggesting that families are brooder houses for producing human beings, trying for maximum numbers per household, but rather that households/families spend large amounts on human-resource development, a large part of which enters into production outside the family and the benefits of which accrue to the individual family member and to society at large. In other words, families, through the grants economy, are contributing a major input to the increased production of goods and services in our economic system.[2] The puzzlement of economists for a number of years over why gross national product increased at a more rapid clip than the rate of increase in input of the traditional factors of production finally gave rise to a new emphasis on human-capital economics. Apparently some began to think that maybe, just maybe, labor was more than the sweat of the brow and that human labor had qualitative dimensions as well.

Gary Becker, among others, has contributed to this development.[3] He identifies one of the dimensions of human-resource development, among others, as decisions about the numbers, timing, and spacing of children. But the numbers are not perhaps the most interesting or important dimension. The developmental dimension as it affects quality of children who, when grown, are the human-resource output of families is even more intriguing. Families are one of the major educational influences even today. Admittedly, a significant part of the educational function has been delegated to agencies outside the family, but the family continues to be a major educational influence in its own right and, in addition, connects its members with educational opportunities outside the family and *pays* for those in large part. I refer here not only to the education of younger members but also to the education, training, and retraining of individual family members of all ages.

Services Produced in Families

Further reflection may be in order about the importance of services rendered within the family, one member to another. Education has already been mentioned. In addition, what about health services, moral-ethical teaching, and attitude development, including trust? I do not believe much attention has been given to the economic worth of the family—either potential or actual—as an active part of the health-care-delivery system. What is known about the economic impact of good or poor nutrition habits learned in substantial part from experiences as a member of a family? Could the family be used more effectively as an educational influence to improve this capability? If so, how? What would be the cost-benefit analysis? Further, what about learning and appreciating the importance of exercise? Could families essentially replace health spas? What would be the savings in use of acute health-care facilities if families did more to fulfill this potential? Could not the family/home serve more widely and more discerningly as a diagnosis center? Are not personal-family resources as well as societal resources being wasted by too great a reliance on doctors for problems that probably never need their attention, thus draining their time and energies from more important tasks? And, of course, what about the role of the family in the furtherance of mental health as well as the more discerning diagnosis of mental-health needs? Naturally, no one in his or her right mind would suggest avoiding professional medical advice and care when needed, but is it not worth considering that perhaps families have an important potential economic impact through their actual or potential delivery of health services?

One service that is difficult to delegate entirely outside the family is that of developing family members' moral and ethical capacities. That is not to say that outside agencies do not contribute—certainly religion plays an important part for many, for instance. However, the development of long-term ethical attitudes and commitments takes place in substantial measure through the home and family environment. What are the economic ramifications of these? For one, the capacity to trust, built partly on one's own ethical code as well as a confidence in one's human environment, is important to the smooth functioning of social activity and institutions and has, I suggest, important economic ramifications too. Without trust, how would the day-to-day affairs of the marketplace take place? How much more would it cost to transact business if explicit checks and balances had to be built in at every turn? We have far to go to quantify the contribution of families even to smooth and lower-cost market transactions.

Further, to what extent is interest in and participation in political affairs affected by attitudes developed in whole or part from experiences and learnings within a family? What in turn is it worth to society to have human resources that are active in nature rather than passive? To what extent might it be speculated that not only is political decision making affected but that economic efficiency is also affected by more active participation in the political processes? In other words, might not government regulation, provision of support services to families, and so on be more finely tuned to human needs because of attitudes acquired in the family which encourage active participation in public decision-making? This is a contribution coming out of families which has a definite economic impact.

Another output, potential and/or actual, of families is the "production" of attitudes among family members that view marital possessions in proper relation to use of resources for human-resource development, maintenance, or conservation. In other words, an ability to see the things of the home and family as means to ends, not as ends. This in turn might have broad economic and social meanings as it worked itself out in a systems sense.

Also economic development, even in a fairly advanced country such as the United States, requires an open attitude toward change. Much of the predisposition toward change probably is an outcome of experience in families, thus an economic contribution of families to the larger society. On the other hand, creative resistance to change sometimes is important too, and this also may be learned in the family; at least that is a potential. Thus the concept of families as active agents for change when change is desirable and the ability to arbitrate between when change is desirable and when it should be resisted (for example, for sake of cultural integrity or other reasons), may be an important economic function of families that we really do not know much about or that we may hardly recognize for that matter.

Time and the Family

Another area in which families make decisions having important economic ramifications for themselves and society is in time allocations such as between paid employment outside versus time spent within the home providing services, time allocated to activities within the family or home and time allocation between maintenance of material inventories (household "stuff") and human-development activities. Further, little is known about the inter-life-cycle effects—that is, the differences that result during later stages of the family life cycle of time-use decisions in a previous stage.

Paid Employment versus Work in the Home

Time allocations between paid employment and time in the home have received increasing attention as the trend for more family members to work outside the home has progressed. Becker, Schultz, Morgan, Helmick, and Metzen, among others, have looked at this phenomenon.[4] Here the important question would seem to be: What differences flow from such decisions? One outcome might be that a better match is struck between skills needed in economic activities of all kinds and inherent abilities—that is, the benefits of specialization and division of labor would be captured to a fuller extent. But at the same time it necessitates several compensating adjustments such as obtaining child care of at least as high a quality as that provided by family members and making chauffering services available. Whether these services are available in the "packages" that serve as substitutes for, say, a woman's—or, for that matter, a man's —services within the family is a matter of local market conditions. But it seems that getting a perfect match of these conditions is difficult in many locations. Nevertheless, the provision of labor services outside the home by more family members means that the family is thereby providing a resource to the larger society *in the present.* The longer term effects are hard to be sure of: If, in fact, the human-resource development within the family is diminished, the quality of human resources of the younger members of families may be lessened, and, in the next generation of workers, a less optimum quality of human resource will be forthcoming that would have obvious economic impact. Clearly, that is not known to be the outcome, but it is important to do more to determine the long-term effects that may result. Many of these effects will be subtle and difficult to measure.

Spending Effects

Another dimension of the out-of-the-home work phenomenon is the greater family incomes that result. This obviously means families may consume more—more services to substitute for those that family members would do in the home if they were not working and more goods and services of other kinds too. Interestingly enough, one recent study seems to cast doubt on the idea that families in which the woman has recently become a paid worker outside the family automatically become "big spenders." Strober and Weinberg found that wives' recent entry in the labor force did not significantly affect decisions to purchase supposedly time-saving durables such as dishwashers and dryers or even such items as TVs, furniture, hobby and recreational items, or vacations or college educations.[5] Such findings, if substantiated with further studies, cast doubt on the idea that families consider wives' earnings as transitory income and/or treat these earnings differently from other income.

Another type of home production that families can and do engage in is that of making "wise" (shrewd) decisions about consumer goods and services. Every time people make purchases at a price advantage, it is effectively an increase in income. And each dollar "earned" through prudent buying is augmented because it is tax-free.[6] Such savings forgone due to time constraints when married women work outside the home may be an unnoted cost of such paid employment. And any time there is a lessening of consumers' guard on the buying side of the market, there is less of a "policing" action in the market and the opportunity for price exploitation is enhanced.

The broad question still remains: What are the spending impacts of families having more family members working in paid employment?

Costs When Families Falter

A possible economic ramification of a negative type is that of the private and societal costs when the family falters or fails. Information about the total costs of divorce, for example, is woefully lacking. The direct costs are fairly clear, but the costs attendant to maintaining two households, extra travel, effects on human-resource development, and other secondary, long-term ramifications are far from clear.

One cannot help but wonder about the realism of families' commitment to single-family residences. Is this an attachment based on a full accounting of advantages and disadvantages, or is it a passion needing containment through admitting cost considerations into the decision frame? Even though families say they much prefer single-family residences, are conditions changing to the extent that this type of housing is a cost that they or society cannot sustain indefinitely? In other words, are families resisting change in this area at very high personal and societal costs?

To what extent can or should the increase in crime be counted as a cost of families' failing to function adequately? Undoubtedly, other influences are at work, but might it not seem realistic to think that increases in crime are at least partially an externality resulting from less than optimum functioning of the family?

Conclusion

Having simply pointed toward some economic dimensions of families, the following are suggested as a partial agenda for investigation of the economic role of families in human-resource development, conservation and maintenance, and allocation:

1. The economic valuation of the educational functions that families perform for their members.
2. The economic contribution (actual or potential) of families as health-care providers or vendors.
3. The "worth" to society of moral and ethical frameworks developed in substantial measure through family experience.
4. The economic ramifications of development of attitudes as a result of family experience leading to political activitism rather than passiveness in political affairs.
5. Development of more awareness of the connections between materialism and human development.
6. The contribution of families in bringing about change and in developing attitudes conducive to assuming the risk associated with change as well as that related to creative resistance to change.
7. Long-term effects on human-resource development and on spending patterns of more family members' engaging in paid employment outside the home.
8. Pay-offs of shrewd consumer decision making both to the individual or family and to society as a brake on price manipulation and on market concentration.
9. Negative effects (costs, both private and societal) when families falter—for example, the total costs of divorce.

Notes

1. Hazel Kyrk, *The Family in the American Economy* (Chicago: University of Chicago Press, 1953), especially chap. 4.

2. See Kenneth E. Boulding, *The Economy of Love and Fear* (Belmont, Calif.: Wadsworth, 1973); see also Gordon E. Bivens, "The Grants Economy and Study of the American Family: A Possible Framework for Trans-disciplinary Approaches," *Home Economics Research Journal* 5(1976):70-78.

3. Gary S. Becker, "A Theory of Marriage," in *Economics of the Family*, ed. T.W. Schultz (Chicago: University of Chicago Press, 1974). The volume by Schultz contains papers from a conference on this topic. See also H. Correa, *The Economics of Human Resources* (Amsterdam: North-Holland, 1963). Although there has recently been a vigorous reaffirmation of the importance of human capital by Schultz, Becker, Correa, and others, early economists too had emphasized an economic analysis of the investment in humans. In the *Wealth of Nations*, Adam Smith stressed the significance of education and included "the acquired and useful abilities of all the inhabitants or members" in his comments on "fixed capital." Alfred

Marshall also emphasized that "the most valuable of all capital is that invested in human beings."

4. Gary S. Becker, "A Theory of Marriage," in *Economics of the Family*, ed. T.W. Schultz (Chicago: University of Chicago Press, 1974); James N. Morgan, Ismail Sirageldin, and Nancy Baerwaldt, *Productive Americans* (Ann Arbor, Mich.: University of Michigan Press, 1966); Sandra J. Helmick and Edward J. Metzen, "Family Employment Intensity and Income Adequacy: A Multi-Sample Analysis," *Journal of Home Economics Research* 2(1977):120-130.

5. Myra H. Strober and Charles R. Weinberg, "Working Wives and Major Family Expenditures," *Journal of Consumer Research* 4(1977):141-147.

6. See, for example, E. Scott Maynes, *Decision-Making for Consumers* (New York: MacMillan, 1976).

Additional References

Bohannan, P. *Divorce and After*. New York: Doubleday, 1970.

Boulding, K.E. *Beyond Economics*. Ann Arbor, Mich.: University of Michigan Press, 1970.

Chiswick, B.R., and O'Neil, June A., *Human Resources and Income Distribution*. New York: W.W. Norton, 1977.

Hill, Rueben. *Family Development in Three Generations*. Cambridge, Mass.: Schenkman, 1970.

Kreps, J.M. "The economics and intergenerational relationships." In *Social Structure and the Family: Generational Relations*, ed. E. Shanas and G.F. Streib. Englewood Cliffs, N.J.: Prentice-Hall, 1965.

Mead, M. "Anomalies in American Postdivorce Relationships." In *Divorce and After*, ed. P. Bohannan. New York: Doubleday, 1970.

Walker, K.E., and Gauger, W.H. *The Dollar Value of Household Work*, Information Bulletin 60, New York State College of Human Ecology. Ithaca, N.Y.: Cornell University, 1973.

Walker, K.E., and Woods, M.E. *Time Use: A Measure of Household Production of Family Goods and Services*. Washington, D.C.: Center for the Family, American Home Economics Association, 1976.

**Part I
Economic Roles of
Wives**

2 The Relative Income Shares of Male and Female Homemakers

R.K. Armey

The relative income of men and women is one of the most controversial issues of income distribution. This issue is complex, and thus it is difficult to make useful generalizations. However, it is possible to make an important distinction, considering the problem from a female perspective, between compensation issues for women in the pecuniary employments as opposed to women in the nonpecuniary employments. This chapter concerns the nonpecuniary employment of women. However, first, it will discuss briefly the pecuniarily employed women.

The "new woman" has come of age. She is making her way in the pecuniary employments. She has served notice that she will no longer acquiesce to traditional rationalizations for compensating her with less-than-equal pay for equal work or for discriminating against her in hiring practices. Feminists have well documented prejudicial hiring practices and unequal pay. They consistently keep faith in women and their ability as they demand that compensation be determined on a quid pro quo basis.[1] They reject the argument that men *need* a higher rate of compensation to support their dependents. Furthermore, they reject and resist the tradition of female dependency. Feminists realize that merit and productivity compensation formulas leave less room for prejudice and discrimination than do "need" formulas. They recognize that merit formulas are not only more equitable but make a greater contribution to productivity than do need formulas. To many of us this is an especially refreshing return to productivity-based compensation principles and to the traditional quid pro quo ethic.

When considering issues of income distribution between men and women, the feminists have done an excellent job of documenting discrimination in the pecuniary employments. One reason for this excellence is that the pecuniary employments are automatically brought under the measuring rod of money. The data are naturally generated, and there is little room for speculation and conjecture. Consequently one finds in that debate realistic and well-documented scientific discourse. Feminists have clearly demonstrated that in the pecuniary employments sex discrimination is a common practice.

The author would like to thank Ms. Susan D. Tipton and Professor Rose Rubin for their helpful comments and suggestions. They are, of course, in no way responsible for the paper's deficiencies.

Feminist efforts have not been so well conceived nor so effective when directed toward the case of women in their chief nonpecuniary occupation—housework. One important reason is that nonpecuniary activity is not naturally brought under the measuring rod of money. Documentation is therefore not natural, and there inevitably is speculation and conjecture. In general, arguments concerning housewives and their relative income share are less professional than those concerning the pecuniary employments. They tend to appear in popular periodicals and fashionable paperbacks rather than in professional journals. However, even when found in professional journals, articles concerning housework are often characterized by misrepresentations and conspiracy theories. The upshot of most of these misrepresentations is the allegation that housewives are uncompensated.

There seems to be a widespread consensus that the housewife is a veritable slave and that there is something of a conspiratorial establishment that abrogates her freedom to chose alternative life styles and compels her to a life of servitude and dependency. It is argued that women are "conditioned" to make involuntary choices contrary to their "real" interests. They end up, according to these scenarios, as manipulated, exploited victims of a cruel system, which does not even recognize their contribution, let alone reward them for it. According to Margaret Benston, "women are an unpaid labor force."[2] A frequently suggested solution to this problem is for husbands to pay their wives a pecuniary salary.[3]

One interesting variation of the theme that housewives are an unpaid labor force is a justification for alimony on the basis that it is "back pay" for uncompensated years of service rendered. It is worth noting that many progressive feminists reject alimony because it perpetuates women's dependency status, a condition generally resisted by the feminist movement. Two additional interesting variations in the argumnet are that housewives do not receive raises and that they enjoy no retirement benefits. The points are simply incorrect.

It is ironic that much of the mischief perpetuated against the issue of housewives' income shares was inspired by a somewhat casual observation attributed to the eminent economist Arthur Cecil Pigou. He observed that, according to generally accepted national income-accounting practices, if a man were to marry his housekeeper, there would be a decrease in the Gross National Product. Pigou's observation was intended merely to illustrate a known weakness in national income accounting—that it does not account well for economic activity not generated through markets and not brought naturally under the measuring rod of money. As a criticism of national income accounting, the point is well taken, if only incidental. Furthermore, there are many activities that are similarly precluded from the national income accounts. In particular, there are do-it-yourself activities done around the home by husbands. Obviously, economists made the judicious decision to confine national income accounting to activity that could be consistently measured. This has always seemed (to me at least) to be an innocent enough choice on their part.

Not everyone agrees that the decision to omit housewives' nonpecuniary employment from national income accounts is innocent. There is a tendency to infer that it is part of a conspiracy to "keep women in their place." For example, Nona Glazer-Malbin states, "Only the low status of women and the disparagement of housework can explain why economists have found estimating the contribution of housework to economic well-being an insoluble problem.[4] She claims that economists have solved a similar problem in the estimation of real-estate value.

John Kenneth Galbraith goes even further with his allegation that the conventional pedagogy keeps women uninformed concerning the contribution of housework to national productivity:

> The labor of women to facilitate consumption is not valued in national income or product. This is of some importance for its disguise; what is not counted is often not noted. For this reason, and aided by the conventional pedagogy as presently observed, it becomes possible for women to study economics without becoming aware of their precise role in the economy. This, in turn, facilitates their acceptance of their role. Were their economic function more explicitly delineated in the current pedagogy, it might invite inconvenient rejection.[5]

Galbraith's version of the conspiracy against women, particularly the housewife, is one of the most colorful and rich scenarios and one of the most widely accepted. He maintains that women have been converted into "cryptoservants" by the economic system that has shaped their attitudes and molded their behavior to fit its needs.[6]

In this conspiracy theory there are two euphemisms that substitute for the conventional "they" or "establishment" that characterize most conspiracy theories. One is "the economic system," as previously mentioned. The other is one of Professor Galbraith's more glamorous rhetorical innovations—"the convenient social virtue," which he says "ascribes merit to any pattern of behavior, however uncomfortable or unnatural for the individual involved, that serves the comfort or well-being of, or is otherwise advantageous for, the more powerful members of the community."[7] According to Galbraith, the economic system and the convenient social virtue convert women to menial personal service.

To summarize, Galbraith contends that powerful members of the economic community regulate the economic system by using the convenient social virtue to create cryptoservants out of housewives who will manage consumption without compensation in order to maintain a high demand for products, the need for which has been created by Madison Avenue's control over the consumer's will by the media. In all of this they are aided by the conventional pedagogy that does not inform the housewife of her precise role in the economy. The particular manner by which we keep the housewife uninformed is by disguise. We do not count her contribution in the national income accounts, and "what is not counted is often not noted."[8] Apparently Professor Galbraith believes the housewife would not note that she scrubbed the floors unless she saw it counted in the Gross National Product.

The cryptoservant is not compensated in Galbraith's scenario. She is compelled to perform menial personal service, and she receives no compensation nor even any credit in the national income accounts. As incredible as this scenario seems, it appears to be widely appreciated by "sophisticated" social critics. It seems that we have come a long way since Pigou uttered his casual observation that housework is not counted in the Gross National Product.

It turns out that, in fact, estimating the value of a housewife's services has not been totally neglected by economists. Galbraith himself points out: "The value of the services of housewives has been calculated, somewhat impressionistically, at roughly one-fourth of total Gross National Product. The average housewife has been estimated (at 1970 wage rates for equivalent employments) to do about $257 worth of work a week or some $13,364 a year."[9] There are various other estimates of the value of housework. Chase Manhattan Bank of New York (in apparant ignorance of how important it is to keep cryptoservants uninformed) estimated that the average housewife works about 100 hours per week at a value of $352 (in 1977 wage rates). They arrived at these figures by multiplying the wage rates of different services housewives perform by the estimated time they spend at each task. [The tasks used were (1) nursemaid, (2) cook, (3) dishwasher, (4) laundress, (5) food buyer, (6) chauffeur, (7) gardner, (8) maintenance person, (9) seamstress, (10) dietician, and (11) practical nurse.][10]

There are many problems related to such estimates that would make them unacceptable for national income-accounting purposes. Galbraith himself points out that the calculations have been impressionistic. These estimates are neither consistent enough nor reliable enough to meet the needs of national income accounting, and conventional pedagogy is all the more responsible for leaving them out. There are three particular and obvious sources of error. The first is that the Chase study valued housework at New York City wages, which would be higher than the national average. A second error is the blatantly sexist substance of Chase's "laundry list."

Women do not do only "women's work," as this list suggests. The third and perhaps greatest error is the tendency to double-count hours spent. For example, a nursemaid to sleeping children may simultaneously be a laundress washing clothes and a dietician planning a menu. Walker and Woods present a well-documented, more realistic estimate of 56 hours per week as well as testimony concerning the contributions made by other members of the household.[11]

Despite all these vagaries, we can consider the Chase study a legitimate effort to measure the nonmeasurable and to generalize about the nongeneralizable. We have with it objective estimates that are useful for certain advocacy and illustrative purposes. Most important, we have testimony concerning the pecuniary value of *real output* contributed by the housewife in her nonpecuniary employment. That takes us back to the question, What accuracy is there in the commonly accepted proposition that the housewife is not compensated for her real-output contributions?

One of the most fascinating cases, from which the generally accepted proposition that housewives are unpaid has emerged, is in a special contest sponsored by Eduard and Doris Bernays and conducted by Babson College in Babson Park, Massachusetts. The purpose of the contest was to find a way to reimburse housewives for their services. According to a newspaper account of the contest, Doris Bernays was quoted as saying, "Since I could not come up with the solution maybe somebody else could."[12] I have no doubt that she is unable to come up with a solution because the problem is illusionary.

The contention that housewives are not compensated for their work, that they are an unpaid labor force, is a classic example of (if I too may indulge in some rhetorical innovation) *money disillusion*. Money disillusion is the opposite of money illusion. Money illusion is a tendency to overestimate real income in consideration of money income. For example, if a person receives an 8-percent increase in his money income in the face of 10 percent inflation, he would if he suffered money illusion ignore the inflation and believe himself to be 8 percent better off. Although this has been a rather common affliction in the past, the conventional pedagogy has educated the general public to the point that money illusion is largely eradicated from public misconception.

As the public has overcome its traditional affliction of money illusion, it has tended to become overly sensitive to the effect of inflation, and there has emerged a new affliction: money disillusion. It is common now to understimate your real income in consideration of your money income. The current trend is for someone who experiences an 8-percent increase in money income along with a 10-percent rate of inflation to believe that he is 2-percent worse off. Not necessarily so! Income earners typically have some portion of their income committed to long-term debt obligations such as mortgage payments. This income is shielded from inflation. Consequently, a person with an 8-percent money income increase and 10-percent inflation might *realistically* understand that he has, *in reality*, no change in his *real* income. Money illusion is a tendency to overestimate real income in relation to pecuniary income. Money disillusion is a tendency to underestimate real income in relation to money income.

The argument that housewives are unpaid labor rests on the observable fact that they receive no money income. Money income is not a good definition of income because it is so easily made illusionary in one direction or another. A more realistic and useful definition of income is the total of real goods consumed and real wealth accumulated. On the basis of that definition, the housewife *is* compensated for her services. Consider the following example as a "mental experiment."[13] We shall assume that both the husband and the wife have an equal responsibility for the family's support. We realize that the internal distribution of goods varies considerably in different households. On the extremes we see some cases where the husband "gets everything" and others where the wife "gets it all." For our example, however, we must assume the most useful possible generalization. I believe that is to assume that the household's real income is equally divided among the wife, husband, and their mutual dependents. Since our discussion specifically concerns the question of compensation for housework and since, as I have earlier indicated, issues of women's pecuniary employment are well covered in other sources, I shall confine my example and my discussion to the nonpecuniarily employed housewife.

In our example, the household's real income derives from three sources: the wife's real output, the husband's pecuniary income, and the husband's real output around the home. We shall do our best to fairly estimate these income sources for a "representative home." We shall try to utilize objective data insofar as it is available. Our aim is to be objective and have "fair" estimates. We do not pretend to have empirical facts because they cannot be had. Consider the household's real income item by item as we exemplify it in our mental experiment.

Item 1: The housewife's real output of "housework." We can use the 1977 update of the Chase Manhattan estimate cited earlier for our example and represent the housewife's contribution to total *real* family income at approximately $18,304 annually ($352 × 52 weeks).

Item 2: The husband's money income deriving from his conventional employment. We shall assume that he is a typical middle-income worker employed for a 40-hour week. He uses his pecuniary income to provide for the family. These externally purchased provisions are especially important since they represent a *real-income base* to which *value is added* through the real product of both the male and the female homemaker. According to the U.S. Bureau of the Census, the median earnings for husbands was $14,144 in 1977.[14]

Item 3: The husband's real output of housework. This item is likely to be the most controversial of the three simply because it is one for which there is no documented study. Chase Manhattan did not add up the value of the husband's housework. Consequently, we have no documented information so we must make a guess. I have asked my friends and I have asked several classes of students. We have generally agreed that husbands typically do about one fourth as much work around the house as the housewife. That includes, for example, cleaning and maintaining automobiles, general household repair, some housework, some cooking, yardwork, nursemaid, chauffeur, little-league coach, and dishwasher.[15] If we assume that one fourth is a reasonable estimate and that the husband's housework has the same monetary value per hour as the wife's housework, then his housework can be valued at $4,576 annually.

By summing items 1, 2, and 3, we can have a representative family with a representative *real* income of $37,024. Of course, we are taking liberties with accepted empirical techniques when we add items 1, 2, and 3. There may be some bias. However, our purpose is to develop an "objective" example concerning a subject for which there are no objective data. We do the best we can to develop a fair representation. At least we can be satisfied that the data are independent of our individual bias or experience. Anyone who would take exception to any or all of the values for items 1, 2, or 3 may do so and assume or find your own values. The argument made here will still stand. It is a "mental experiment."

The wife's contribution to that total real income is $18,304. If the husband and the wife have an equal responsibility for the household's support and if the family's real income is equally divided between the husband and wife, she is not only paid for her labor, but in our "mental experiment" she is almost perfectly fairly compensated. She has provided about half the family income. Thus she has fulfilled her responsibility to provide half the support. She receives real income of $18,512 and she contributes $18,304. She is overpaid by $208. Of course, this is only an example. We have generalized about a subject concerning which generalizations cannot be made. Each household is a unique entity that experiences different relative contributions to total income and different relative levels of consumption between the husband and wife. Still, even though our mental experiment has only the most tenuous empirical validity, it is certainly more realistic and accurate than the complete misrepresentation in the commonly accepted generalization the "housewives are an unpaid labor force."

There are other points that can be addressed briefly. The contention that the housewife does not experience pay increases is equally false. Every time the husband's wage increases (in constant dollars), the family income increases, and likewise her share. Furthermore, as the family grows older, child care becomes less of a burden, and the household accumulates labor-saving devices such as vacuums, dishwashers, and food processors. Consequently, her workload decreases as her income increases, and, in short, her life gets better.[16]

It is widely contended that housewives receive no retirement benefits. Not so! They are the largest single class of noncontributing adult social-security beneficiaries. In fact, a pecuniarily employed woman has the choice to take, upon retirement, her paid benefits or one half the benefit paid her husband. Presumably she will take the larger benefit. In addition, most households have accumulated wealth, vested pension funds, and private insurance plans that provide the widow or dependent wife with retirement benefits. That these benefits are often not sufficient to meet her needs is certain, but they do exist and largely in amounts that are the consequence of the woman and her husband's determination.

The final and bottom-line argument is, What if she gets divorced or widowed and is left with no means of support nor any marketable skills? That is, of course, the meanest of all conditions. Unfortunately, this is a chance she takes when she elects marriage and nonpecuniary employment. Admittedly, her decision may be misinformed and romanticized. It is often a conditioned choice, but it is a choice. The upshot is that if one chooses to be dependent, one places one's destiny in someone else's hands. The potential consequences of these choices are seldom fully explained to children who are making lifetime contracts that are not enforceable under the law. It is ironic that women tend to be the greatest advocates of love and marriage even though they tend to be the institution's most hapless victims.

When a man and woman remain married until "death do us part," the arrangement is generally equitable and mutually beneficial. There are serious cases of wife and husband abuse, but they are exceptional, and if a couple remains together, one must accept that they consider this choice to be the best (or at least, least worst) among alternatives. Widowhood leaves women with difficult financial problems. However, there are special provisions for women in social security, and they do have some provision under private insurance and retirement plans. Women still suffer some discrimination in inheritance laws where their contributions to the family's accumulated wealth are not recognized. These injustices can be eliminated, and progress is being made as the feminist movement makes its impact felt in legislation and court decisions. In estate cases the courts are beginning to recognize the housewife's contribution. It turns out that a woman is financially better off becoming a widow rather than becoming divorced. The advice to shoot your husband rather than divorce him is good financial advice, assuming you can get away with it.

The greatest economic inequities suffered by women result from divorce. Here the husband and wife have made an unwritten agreement. He agrees to specialize in a pecuniary employment while she agrees to specialize in a nonpecuniary employment. They agree to their mutual support. He develops marketable skills. She does not. His skills make him financially independent. Hers do not. If they divorce, she is left with no means of pecuniary support, or at least only the most nominal of marketable skills. Furthermore, she has a broken and limited "employment" record. Even though, as we have shown, she irrefutably has been compensated during her married years, she suffers a handicap in efforts to support herself after divorce. She works for herself but she also works for the family. If she gets a divorce, she loses her husband and her real-income base. The husband loses the wife's value-added output. The husband's loss is more easily replaced than the wife's. He must simply self-employ that production. She must meet social-institutional employment conditions that she avoided in her nonpecuniary employment.

Society has traditionally imputed to the ex-husband a continued responsibility for the wife's support through her alimony that continued until she remarried. That practice is largely unacceptable today except in cases of the very wealthy. The decreasing acceptability of alimony derives not only from male opposition but also feminist opposition. The reason for male opposition is fairly obvious; they do not want to pay. The reason for feminist opposition to alimony is less obvious. To the feminist, alimony is objectionable because it represents a continued acceptance of dependent status for women. Alimony denies a woman's independence. It also reinforces the public misconception that women do not need equal pay for equal work with men. Alimony is, in short, sexist.

In effect, the primary economic problem of divorced women is occupational rehabilitation. Divorce in general, but no-fault divorce in particular, is making full-time housework an obsolete occupation. One partial solution to this dilemma is for the former employer (the husband) and/or the state to assume some responsibility for training and educational benefits that will help to upgrade the housewife's marketable skills. This is particularly equitable for women whose husbands have advanced educations often deriving from the wives' past assistance and sacrifice. In effect, husbands accumulate occupational capital assets and wives do not. A property settlement should recognize those assets and make provision for the wife's comparable attainment. It would be equitable for the court to make a special assessment against the husband for that purpose. In addition to the equity of job-retraining settlements, there is an efficiency argument that should be fairly obvious. If the independent woman is trained and skilled, she will be a more productive member of the community. Social benefit will include fewer female-headed poverty households and more female-headed taxpaying households.

In most divorce cases child custody is still given to the woman. That is changing but very slowly. So long as the woman has child custody, the husband has a personal interest in her economic well-being. She will provide at least half the children's pecuniary support and the largest part of their overall support. If she is happy and prosperous, the children will be likewise. That is in the man's interest.

If we recognize that the wife has a past record of nonpecuniary employment where she worked in large part for her husband and contributed to his support and if we recognize that divorce constitutes her losing her job, we can then suggest that she receive a variation of severance pay for her discontinued employment. Severance pay is not an uncommon practice in the pecuniary employments, and it is certainly recognized as an equitable contribution of a past employer to facilitate the relocation of the former employee. It would seem consistent then for the ex-husband to be assessed a certain amount of severance pay (as opposed to alimony) based on the value of past output and years of service by the ex-wife. In order to achieve equitable treatment, the work that has been done by Chase Manhattan and others in assessing the value of housework can be effectively used to estimate proper amounts. Certainly, there must be a heavy reliance on the court's discretion, but that is always so in divorce cases. The fact is we do have some objective data with which to formulate estimated values. The recommended severance pay is more desirable than the historic alimony for two reasons. First, it will be assessed for a limited amount and time period, commensurate with the length of marriage, family size and age, and husband's ability to pay. Second, rather than to endorse the women's dependent status as in the case of alimony, the severance pay recommendation recognizes and encourages a new independence status.

Notes

1. One of my favorite feminist slogans illustrates the confidence that contemporary women have in their ability to compete with men on an equal-pay-for-equal-work basis. It says, "A woman must do twice as much and do it twice as well as a man in order to get half the credit. Fortunately, that is not hard to do."

2. Margaret Benston, "The Political Economy of Woman's Liberation," *Monthly Review* 21 (1969):13-27.

3. Nona Glazer-Malbin, "Housework," *Signs* 1 (1976):920.

4. Ibid., p. 909.

5. John Kenneth Galbraith, *Economics and the Public Purpose* (Boston: Houghton Mifflin, 1973), p. 33.

6. Ibid., pp. 33, 37.

7. Ibid., p. 30.

8. Ibid., p. 33.

9. Ibid., p. 33. Professor Galbraith is quoting figures from Ann Crittenden Scott, "The Value of Housework, For Love or Money," *MS Magazine*, July 1972.

10. The data of the Chase Manhattan Bank study were obtained from Milton Spencer, *Contemporary Economics*, 2d ed. (New York: Worth Publishers, 1974), p. 127. The original study listed figures using wage rates for 1973. The 1977 figures were from an update of the Chase Manhattan Bank study by the American Council of Life Insurance, quoted from Sylvia Porter, "The Million Dollar Housewife," *Dallas Morning News*, September 20, 1978.

11. Kathryn E. Walker and Margaret E. Woods, *Time Use: A Measure of Household Production of Family Goods and Services* (Washington, D.C.: Center for the Family, American Home Economics Association, 1976). A discussion of their work is in the chapter appendix.

12. *Chicago Tribune*, July 14, 1978.

13. The concept of a "mental experiment" is borrowed from Albert O. Hirschman who used it to describe his seminal work, *The Strategy of Economic Development* (New Haven: Yale University Press, 1961), pp. 104-106. Hirschman believed that by identifying the discussion as a "mental experiment," he could prevent readers from overgeneralizing his peculiar example. His intent was rather to illustrate the principle. I have the same hope and intent even though I realize that the tendency to overgeneralize a quasi-empirical example is no more likely to be overcome by me here than by Hirschman there.

14. U.S. Bureau of the Census, *Statistical Abstract of the United States: 1978*, 99th ed. (Washington, D.C.: Government Printing Office, 1978), p. 423, table no. 685.

15. See Walker and Woods, *Time Use*, and appendix 2A for information on male participation in housework.

16. Support for this point is in appendix 2A and in Walker and Woods, *Time Use*.

Appendix 2A
Household Time Use

In his *Economics and the Public Purpose*, John Kenneth Galbraith chastises the economics profession for its failure to develop an adequate analysis of the internal economics of the home.[1] He further suggests that our failure to do so is in accordance with our "instrumental function" as outlined in the paper. He then points out that despite our design to not measure the value of housework in order to disguise the housewife's cryptoservant role, the value of housework has been impressionistically measured. This impressionistic measurement pops up again and again. However, it always seems to take the form of a pecuniary update of the time-use data in the Chase Manhattan Bank study.[2]

It turns out that one reason we might excuse the economics profession for its failure to study the internal economics of the home is that the job is already being done and done well by scholars in home economics. Home economics is largely a misunderstood and underappreciated discipline. The quality of scholarship in the field is excellent and clearly superior to what is found in other fields doing "impressionistic" measurement of issues not central to their scope. The contrast is dramatic between the Chase time-use study and one done by Kathryn E. Walker and Margaret E. Woods for the American Home Economics Association.[3]

Walker and Woods employed a team of trained interviewers to conduct an elaborate survey of a scientifically selected sample of 1,296 families in Syracuse, New York, for the period 1967-1968. The sample was chosen from a list of 50,000 families. Data were collected by personal interview with wives because "the wife was considered to be the person most informed about the household work of all workers in the family."[4] Walker and Woods designated 13 different work activities and found that the average time spent on all activities by all family members was 11.1 hours a day and 77.7 hours a week; considerably less than the 100 hours a week attributed to the housewife alone in the Chase study. Some additional information from the Walker and Woods study is of interest and is summarized below.

The average total housework for all workers in homes where the wife is not employed is 11.1 hours a day. This ranges from 7.2 hours for families with no children to 17.4 hours for families with 7-9 children.

The average total housework for all workers where the wife is employed is 8.7 hours a day. This ranges from 5.0 hours where there are no children to 13.0 hours where there are 5-6 children. The average total housework done by employed wives ranges from 3.7 hours a day with no children to 6.3 hours with 5-6 children.

The average total housework done by nonemployed housewives is 8.0 hours a day for 56 hours a week, considerably less than the 100 hours reported by the Chase study. This ranges from 5.7 hours a day for families with no children to 9.4 hours for families with 7-9 children.

The average total housework done by husbands in households where the wife is not employed is 1.6 hours a day, 20 percent of the average total housework done by the nonemployed wife. This figure tends to support as reasonable the 25-percent figure used in this chapter. The husband's involvement ranges from 1.4 hours a day when there are no children to 2.0 hours when there are 7-9 children. That is, of course, in addition to his regular work day of approximately 8 hours.[5]

One final point is worth noting. As the children grow older, the average total housework diminishes. This point was made in this chapter and is supported by the Walker-Woods study in which they determined that average total housework went from 12.4 hours a day when the youngest child was under one year of age to 10.8 hours when the youngest child was from 12-17 years of age. They further determined that as the youngest child grew older, the children's share of total housework increased and the mother's share decreased.[6]

The Walker-Woods study suggests that the Chase Manhattan Bank study overestimates the housewife's contributions to total family goods and services, at least with respect to time use. It also demonstrates that the discipline of home economics is doing a thorough and scholarly job of studying the internal economics of the home.

Notes

1. John Kenneth Galbraith, *Economics and the Public Purpose* (Boston: Houghton Mifflin, 1973).

2. The data from the Chase Manhattan study are summarized in Milton Spencer, *Contemporary Economics*, 2d ed. (New York: Worth Publishers, 1974), p. 127.

3. Kathryn E. Walker and Margaret E. Woods, *Time Use: A Measure of Household Production of Family Goods and Services* (Washington, D.C.: Center for the Family, American Home Economics Association, 1976).

4. Ibid., p. 10-11.

5. Ibid., p. 56.

6. Ibid., p. 50.

3

The Two-Income Family in Middletown, 1924-1978

Bruce A. Chadwick and
C. Bradford Chappell

Working Wives

A dramatic transformation in family finances has occurred. Recent estimates indicate that both spouses work in nearly half of all marriages.[1] According to a recent study, "the increasing labor force participation of women is one of the most significant transformations of the American social structure to have occurred since the end of World War II."[2] Similar concern about the impact of wives' working on family life is expressed in a recent book which identified the two-paycheck family as "the great revolution of our times"

> Eli Ginzin, the Columbia University specialist in human resources who has advised every President of the United States since Franklin Delano Roosevelt, believes that the employment of women outside the home is the most important social change of the twentieth century, more important than the rise of Communism or the European Common Market.[3]

Although some change in the number of wives in the labor force has occurred, the actual extent and its consequences remain largely a topic of speculation. A replication of the Middletown Community Study provides an opportunity to chart the changes in married women's participation in the labor force between 1920 and 1978 in a typical midwestern community.[4]

The Lynds collected information from a sample of married women with at least one child between the ages of 6 and 18 and found that 34 percent had worked outside the home for money during the previous five years. Obviously this figure is an inflated estimate of the percent of working wives with children since it accumulates those who worked at any time during the five years (1920-1924), but it does indicate that a substantial number of the married women in Middletown were working during this period. Comparable data were collected for the five-year period 1973-1977 in order to assess the degree of change.

The research reported herein was supported by the "Middletown III" project, which is funded by National Science Foundation Grant No. SOC 75-13580. The investigators are Theodore Caplow, Howard M. Bahr, and Bruce A. Chadwick.

Not only does it appear that more married women have entered the labor force, but values supporting their working have also emerged. Magazines, television, and other mass-media presentations proclaim that women have come a long way in the world of work. The implication is that most of the change in public values concerning working wives has occurred rather recently. While this may be true concerning discrimination in types of occupations available to women, the reduction of differences in salary, and the removal of restrictions to promotion, it appears from the Lynds's observations that the change in values concerning women leaving the home for the labor force was largely accomplished by 1920. In 1891 the editor of Middletown's daily newspaper revealed the general community attitude when he proclaimed that "it is true that qualities inherent in the nature of women impede their progress as a wage-earner . . . . Women are uniformly timid and are under a disadvantage in the struggle for a livelihood."[5] Prior to World War I, the rule in Middletown was that when a working woman married, she automatically lost her job. As the industrial revolution attracted women into the factory, a public outcry about the evils of such behavior occurred. An example is a statement made by the state factory inspector in 1900, precipitated by his observation of women laboring in the factories:

> It is a sad comment on our civilization when young women prefer to be employed where they are compelled to mingle with partially clad men, doing the work of men and boys, for little more than they would receive for doing the work usually alotted to women in the home . . . . [One fears] the loss of all maidenly modesty and those qualities which are so highly prized by the true man . . . .[6]

Eventual acceptance of women's involvement in the economy of Middletown is evident in the appearance in 1920 of two businesswomen's clubs founded on the idea of "Better business women for a better business world." Additional support for the idea that values supporting working women had arrived in Middletown by the 1920s is the finding that nearly all the girls in the Middletown high school reported in a survey that they intended to work following graduation. Only 3 percent indicated that they did not expect to do so.[7]

Lynd observed that some husbands were emotionally threatened by their wives' working, as they felt it reflected negatively on their abilities to provide for their families. But he also noted that such feelings were mainly back eddies in a current flowing in the other direction; flowing in the direction of acceptance of the employment of wives and mothers.

An examination of the Lynds's data suggests that the major revolution concerning women's entering the labor force occurred between 1890 and 1920 rather than recently, as many journalists and social scientists have contended. It appears that in Middletown at the turn of the century women sought full-time employment despite values to the contrary, and that as their numbers increased, public values became more supportive. The information gathered in 1977 and 1978 permits the assessment of the change of married women in the labor force since 1920 to test these hypotheses.

Family Expenditures

The wife-mother's exit from the home into the factory, bank, restaurant, and so on, has created both stresses and opportunities for herself and her family. The advantages are perceived to be primarily economic as two incomes should be able to support a higher standard of living. But the question has been raised as to how much family income is actually increased by a working wife when additional expenses, including child care, eating meals out, and state and federal taxes are subtracted. In addition, the question of how the extra income, if there is any, is utilized by the family is frequently asked.

Very little has been published as to whether two-income families spend their income in ways different from single-income families. The Lynds collected information about the amount of income spent on 16 goods and services by 100 working-class families, including 38 with a working wife. The expenditures included housing, automobile, insurance, church and charity contributions, union dues, furniture, and recreation. These data permit a comparison between the expenditures of two-income families and single-income families in 1923 and similar information obtained in 1977 will allow the identification of changes in spending patterns that have occurred during the last fifty years. Thus the second objective of this chapter is to identify differences in spending patterns for two- and single-paycheck families and to establish whether such patterns have changed from 1923 to 1977.

Happiness and Satisfaction

Considerable interest has been expressed about the effects of a wife-mother's employment on the psychological and social well-being of the wife herself as well as on her husband and children. On the one hand, it frequently is argued that working gives a woman an opportunity to develop her talents, to expand her social contacts beyond the immediate family, and to break the boredom of being trapped in the home. On the other hand, a few have questioned the negative effects of the pressures of high-responsibility employment and the drudgery of unskilled jobs on the mental and physical health of working wives.

Research has been conducted as to who are the happiest with their lives in general and with their marriages in particular: working wives or housewives. In a review of studies conducted during the 1950s and 1960s, Burke and Weir concluded that housewives were slightly more happy, satisfied, and adjusted in their marriages than were working wives.[8] But it was hinted that the effects of a working wife affected working-class and business-class families differently as the gap in happiness between working-class housewives and those in the labor force was significantly larger than for business or middle-class wives. Although the Lynds did not report data testing the notion that housewives were happier than working wives, their descriptions of business- and working-class families are consistent with the idea. The Lynds felt that the happy working-class family was an exception because the struggle for economic survival soured the marital relationship. According to the Lynds, most employed wives defined their work as a necessary evil rather than as liberation from the home. But since systematic observations were not reported, the unhappy working wife of 1923 is only speculation, and perhaps if the Lynds had interviewed a sufficient number of working wives, their overall impressions might have been altered. While the changes in the impacts of a working wife between 1923 and 1977 will be tentative, we will examine current levels of happiness and satisfaction in Middletown for both husbands and wives.

Several recent studies refute the happy-housewife finding as they have found that working wives are happier. In a study of 189 married couples in Ontario, Canada, Burke and Weir discovered that working wives were more satisfied with their marriages and reported that their emotional and physical well-being was higher than that of housewives.[9] Ferree interviewed a sample of 135 working-class women in Massachusetts during late 1974 and obtained similar results.[10] She tested the theory that lower-class housewives are happier and better adjusted than their working counterparts because of the unrewarding occupations open to such women. It was hypothesized that women find housework more enjoyable, or at least less distasteful, than boring factory work, washing dishes, waiting on tables, and similar work. Ferree's results contradicted the expected findings as the employed lower-class women in her sample were happier and felt themselves better off than the full-time housewives.[11] Interestingly, it was discovered that those working-class women who worked part time were the happiest of all. It seems that they have the best of both worlds: adequate time to do their housework, the opportunity to get out of the house, plus extra income. Ferree concluded that employment was more liberating than alienating for most of the working-class women she studied.[12]

Orden and Bradburn and Bahr and Day discovered an important intervening variable affecting the relationship between a wife's working and marital satisfaction.[13] Orden and Bradburn analyzed data collected from a sample drawn in several major cities and found that if the wife worked by mutual choice of husband and wife, both were happier than if she worked in spite of one of the spouse's objections.

These more recent studies have reported working women superior in happiness, but the samples have been small, and the differences between working wives and housewives have tended to be equally small. Studies using large national samples have found that housewives and working wives are similar in their perceptions of their marriages and other aspects of their life situation. Campbell examined a national sample of 736 married women and concluded that employment outside the home had no influence on satisfaction with marriage and life.[14] Wright analyzed six national surveys conducted between 1971 and 1976 and found similar results.[15] There were no significant differences between housewives and working wives in their estimates of their marriages, family lives, and lives in general. He suggests that the image of the confused, isolated, and lonely housewife is just as much a myth as is the image of the satisfied, fulfilled working wife. The evidence from these national surveys is quite convincing that employment has limited effect on married women's general happiness, satisfaction, or adjustment.

Although they have not received as much attention, husbands indicate that the impact of a working wife on their happiness is quite different from the effects on their wife's happiness. Not surprisingly, most studies have found that a husband with a working wife perceives his marriage as less happy and his life less satisfying than does the husband whose wife stays home. Probably the wife who works outside the home does not provide the attention and services for her husband that a full-time housewife does. Also some husbands probably feel threatened in their position as head of the family by a working wife. In a study of husbands in Florida, Axelson found that husbands whose wives did not work were happier than those whose wives were in the labor force.[16] Similar results were obtained by Burke and Weir who discovered that professional men with working wives reported poorer health, lower marital happiness, and less satisfaction with life than did professional men married to housewives.[17]

An exception to the neglected-husband syndrome was reported by Campbell who examined the marital satisfaction of a national sample of married couples.[18] He found no difference in the marital happiness of husbands with working wives and those whose wives were in the home. Finally, as mentioned earlier, Orden and Bradburn indicated that if both husband and wife agreed that she should work, then they were as happy with their marriage as were couples where the wife was a homemaker.[19]

In an effort to contribute to the limited data concerning the perceptions of husbands of working wives, we will contrast the marital, occupational, and general life satisfaction of husbands and wives from families where the wife works to those where she is a full-time homemaker. Where possible, changes and trends apparent in Middletown from 1923 to 1977 will be identified.

Methods

The information about Middletown families was collected in three different surveys. The first was a direct replication of the Lynds's interviews with 122 working-class wives and 44 business-class wives who had at least one child at home between the ages of 6 and 19. To obtain comparable data, we interviewed a similar sample during the summer of 1978. A systematic random sample of 2,192 *married* women was drawn from the Middletown City Directory. A letter was sent to each woman explaining the purpose for the study. A reply postcard was enclosed for her to indicate whether she had a child of the specified age and whether she was willing to be interviewed. Of the original sample, 265 women replied that they qualified, and of this number, 178 agreed to be interviewed. Those who expressed a willingness to participate were interviewed.

The 1,583 women who did not return the postcard were telephoned, the study explained, their eligibility ascertained, and the eligibles were invited to be interviewed. Of those telephoned, 518 were eligible, and 155 agreed to be interviewed. The overall response rate was 42 percent; 793 of the 2,192 women selected were eligible, and 333 were interviewed.

The interviews were conducted by six well-trained, mature, married women. The interview schedule used by the Lynds in 1924 was replicated as closely as possible. Employment was determined by asking, "Have you worked full time outside the home at any time during the past five years?" Expenditures were ascertained by this item: "We are interested in the different lifestyles people have in Middletown. Would you please try to estimate how much your family spent last year either for the whole year or for the month for the goods and services listed on this card?"

The second source of data was a mail questionnaire study of women over the age of 18 in Middletown during the spring of 1978. A systematic random sample of 1,006 women was selected from women listed in the 1977 Middletown City Directory. From the sample, 113 were eliminated because they had died or had moved and left no forwarding address. Four follow-ups, including a postcard and three additional copies of the questionnaires, were sent to encourage participation. The final response rate after five mailings over a three-month period was 55 percent; 491 completed questionnaires from 893 eligible women. The questionnaire elicited information about the work experience of those with employment, feelings about the marriage of the married women and their feelings of general happiness with life.

The third source of data was a mail questionnaire study of adult men in Middletown conducted during the spring of 1978. A systematic random sample of 651 men was selected from the Middletown City Directory. Of the sample, 94 were eliminated because they were inaccessible due to death or residential mobility. The follow-up techniques described previously were employed. The final response rate was 39 percent as 215 of the 521 eligible men completed the questionnaire. The questionnaire obtained information about the men's perceptions of general life satisfactions, their feelings about their marriage if married, and their attitudes about their employment.

Both the women's and men's questionnaires included the following two items concerning general and marital happiness: "Taking all things together, how would you say things are these days—would you say that you are very happy, happy, not too happy, pretty unhappy or very unhappy?" and "How do you feel about your relationship with your wife/husband?" The item "How much satisfaction do you get from your family life?" was included in the men's questionnaire only. The response rates for these studies are quite low but were obtained after extensive call-backs and follow-ups. It was felt that any additional pressure on potential respondents would create a severe negative community reaction. In spite of the low response rates, comparisons of several demographic characteristics, education, occupation, income and marital status, with census data indicate that the samples are reasonably representative of the specific populations they were selected from.

Findings

The results from the interviews with married women with children concerning their participation in the labor force for working- and business-class families are presented in table 3-1. The 44 percent of the working-class wives who worked during the period 1920-1924 was somewhat of a surprise.

Table 3-1

Middletown Housewives Holding Full-time Outside Jobs during 1920-1924 and 1973-1977, by Social Class

| | Percent Who Have Worked | | | | | |
| | Working Class[b] | | Business Class[c] | | | |
Period	N	Percent	N	Percent	X^2	P
1920-1924[a]	124	44	40	3	23.9	.001
1973-1977	141	48	192	42	7.7	.01

[a]Robert S. Lynd and Helen M. Lynd, *Middletown* (New York: Harcourt, Brace and World, 1929), p. 270.

[b]The difference between working class in 1920-1924 and 1973-1977 is significant at the .05 level, $X^2 = 5.0$.

[c]The difference between business class in 1920-1924 and 1973-1977 is significant at the .001 level, $X^2 = 22.8$.

Although the increase from 44 percent in 1920-1924 to 48 percent in 1973-1977 is statistically significant, it is a very modest change. It seems that the industrial revolution that swept through Middletown at the turn of the century had attracted the vast majority of Middletown families into a wage-earning lifestyle by 1920. For the working class, employment in the factory provided a higher standard of living than farming but tended to be unpredictable. Factory workers were laid off with regularity for a variety of reasons, including oversupply of goods, weather (too hot to make glass jars), illness, injury, and slowed worker productivity. There were very few buffers such as unions and unemployment insurance to mitigate unemployment, and public-assistance programs were nonexistent in Middletown at this time. It appears that the most common means for the working class to cope with the uncertainty and financial crisis created by periodic unemployment was for the wife to work. The pernicious working-class unemployment seems to have created an influx of married women into the labor force between 1890 and 1920, as evidenced by the 44 percent of the married women who had worked during the 1920-1924 period.

Although a significant proportion of working-class wives were in the labor force by the 1920-1924 period, business-class wives still had not concerned themselves with family economics. Only one business-class wife in the Lynds's sample had worked outside the home during that period, and, not surprisingly, her husband was the only business-class husband to have been unemployed. The comment to the Lynds of one business-class wife illustrates the lack of concern of many such wives about financial matters: "I never let my husband tell me anything about business matters" (p. 126). It is obvious from table 3-1 that business-class wives have since adopted the employment pattern of working-class wives. The increase from 3 percent to 42 percent in 1973-1977 represents a dramatic shift in behavior and almost closes the gap in employment between working- and business-class wives. The more recent trend for business-class women to enter the labor force while no more dramatic than the earlier flight from the home by working-class wives probably has been more visible as business-class wives have been studied much more frequently. The fact that working-class wives were the first to enter the world of work, coupled with social scientists' concentrating their studies on business-class or professional women, probably has contributed to the perception of wives' leaving the home for full-time work as a recent phenomenon.

The data indicate that a working wife's contribution to the family income has significantly increased during the past fifty years. In 1924, for the 100 working-class families that the Lynds interviewed, a working wife increased the family's income by 20 percent, $1,274 to $1,525. In 1978 a working wife expanded the income of the average working-class family 36 percent, $14,543 to $19,756, and the average business-class family's income by 38 percent, $19,557 to $26,905. Greater access to higher status jobs, higher pay, and seniority benefits have all contributed to the substantial increase in a working wife's income in relationship to her husband's income. Thus the economic benefits in terms of gross income of a working wife are greater today than fifty years ago.

The data about expenditures for selected goods and services by working-class families reveal only relatively minor differences between single- and two-income families. If we were constructing the list of expenditures today, we would have deleted some of these included by the Lynds and added others. But in order to assess change in spending patterns, we replicated the 1923 list. It should be noted that the percent of family income spent on these goods and services was almost the same in 1977 as it was in 1923, that is, 35 percent.

The percentages of family income spent on the sixteen goods and services are presented in table 3-2. Although the differences between single- and double-income families are relatively small, several are statistically significant. Statistical significance was achieved because of the large variance in at least one of the groups, even though the means were very similar. In 1924 the working-class family with two incomes tended to spend a higher percent of their income on consumer goods and services such as

Table 3-2
Percent of Family Income Spent on Selected Goods and Services by Working-Class Families in 1923 and 1977

| | 1923 | | 1977 | |
| | Working Wife (N = 38) | Housewife (N = 61) | Working Wife (N = 56) | Housewife (N = 85) |
Goods and Services				
Auto	3.5	4.3[a]	10.4	11.4[a]
Book	.1	.1	.3	.3
Charity	.4	.7[a]	.3	.6[a]
Church	1.6	1.4	1.1	1.8[a]
Concerts, lectures, and so on	.04	.03	.1	.1
Furniture	3.4	3.0[a]	2.6	3.5
House	20.1	15.9	9.8	10.6
Labor unions	.2	.2	.7	.6[a]
Life insurance	3.5	4.3[a]	2.1	1.8[a]
Lodges	.5	.3[a]	.1	.1
Music lessons	1.0	.4[a]	.1	.2[a]
Newspaper, and so on	1.1	.9[a]	.6	.5
Other clubs	.1	.1	.1	.1
Recreation	2.5	2.3	1.4	1.6[a]
Music, stereo, and so on	.1	.1	.4	.4
Vacation	.3	.5[a]	2.4	2.1[a]
Totals	38.4	34.5	32.5	35.7

[a]Significant at .05 level using F ratio to test difference of means.

lodges, music lessons, and newspapers, while the single-income family contributed more to charity. Another significant difference was the single-income family's attempting to provide security by life insurance that could be borrowed from during the times of unemployment and that provided for the family in case of the death of the wage-earner. The differences in expenditure between the single- and double-income working class families appear to have lessened by 1977. The two-income family's tendency to spend more on consumer goods and services has disappeared. Expenditures for life insurance have been reversed as in 1923 single-income families spent more on insurance while in 1977 the opposite was the case. The one trend that has persisted is the single-income family's financial support of charity and religious organizations. Although there were small differences, an overall examination of the expenditure data reveals that in 1923 and in 1977, working-class families spent about the same percentages of their income on the sixteen selected goods and services, regardless of whether they were a single- or double-income family.

The information concerning whether working wives and their husbands are happier than housewives and their mates was obtained from the women's and men's surveys. The results for general happiness, marital satisfaction, and family satisfaction are presented in tables 3-3, 3-4 and 3-5. The differences in happiness for neither wives of business- nor working-class men are statistically significant, although most are in the direction of happier working wives. This similarity in satisfaction between working wives and housewives is consistent with the findings from recent national studies.

In every case, husbands of housewives reported that they were happier than husbands with working wives. Although only three of the six differences achieved statistical significance, the data strongly suggest that men married to full-time housewives are more satisfied with life in general and derive greater satisfaction from their marriages and family life.

The differences in happiness were greater for the business-class husbands as two of the three differences were significant. The business-class husbands may resent the decrease in spouse services and the assault on their ability to provide for their families more than do the working-class husbands because a working wife for someone of their status is a relatively recent phenomenon. Many business-class families with a working wife are the first of their family or peer group to do so. Alternately, it is suspected that the working-class husbands have accepted the likelihood that their wives will work as their mothers probably worked as do many of the wives of their friends.

Discussion

The foregoing results indicate that change in married women's participation in the labor force during the past couple of decades has not been as rapid as

Table 3-3
General Happiness of Married Men and Women in Middletown, by Working Wife and Social Class in 1978

| | Men | | | | Women | | | |
| | Business Class[a] | | Working Class | | Business Class | | Working Class | |
Happiness	Housewife (N = 34)	Working Wife (N = 52)	Housewife (N = 86)	Working Wife (N = 42)	Housewife (N = 40)	Working Wife (N = 100)	Housewife (N = 38)	Working Wife (N = 89)
Very happy	47	17	28	23	35	41	32	27
Pretty happy	47	77	53	67	60	50	58	66
Not too happy								
Pretty unhappy	6	6	19	9	5	9	11	7
Very unhappy								
Totals	100	100	100	99	100	100	101	100

[a]Difference is significant at .05 level, $X^2 = 9.1$.

Table 3-4
Satisfaction with Marital Relationship of Married Men and Women in Middletown, by Working Wife and Social Class in 1978

Marital Satisfaction	Men				Women			
	Business Class		Working Class[a]		Business Class		Working Class	
	Housewife (N = 36)	Working Wife (N = 52)	Housewife (N = 36)	Working Wife (N = 42)	Housewife (N = 40)	Working Wife (N = 98)	Housewife (N = 38)	Working Wife (N = 89)
Very satisfied	65	60	78	57	50	62	45	54
Satisfied	30	33	14	41	45	31	45	38
Neutral								
Dissatisfied	6	8	9	22	5	7	11	8
Very Dissatisfied								
Totals	100	100	100	100	100	100	101	100

[a]Significant at .001 level, $X^2 = 26.2$.

Table 3-5
Satisfaction with Family Life of Married Men in Middletown, by Working Wife and Social Class in 1978

Family Satisfaction	Business Class[a]		Working Class	
	Housewife (N = 33)	Working Wife (N = 52)	Housewife (N = 36)	Working Wife (N = 41)
A great deal	85	54	75	53
Quite a bit	12	33	19	29
Some				
A little	3	14	6	17
None				
Totals	100	101	100	99

[a]Significant at .05 level, $X^2 = 8.8$.

frequently assumed. Working-class wives in Middletown worked almost as frequently in the early 1920s as they do today. On the other hand, the recent entrance of business-class wives into the world of work is a significant change. Married women's movement out of the home and into the labor force is a case of where the working class was the vanguard of change who has been followed by the business class. Since the initial surge of working-class wives into the labor force at the turn of the century, the number has risen only slightly, and if business-class women are following the same pattern, their participation in the labor force should slow down considerably. Overall, there has been a trend for married women having employment outside the home, and the number will probably continue to increase, but the change is certainly not of the catastrophic level portrayed in the media.

The examination of the contribution a working wife makes to family income revealed that there has been a significant increase in women's earning power since 1920. Today women have greater access to higher status and higher paying jobs, are protected by legislation promising equal pay for equal work, and have earned seniority on the job, all of which have increased a working wife's share of the family income. It is expected that this trend will continue until a working wife's share approaches that of her husband.

Because a working wife can increase family income by nearly 40 percent, it was anticipated that two-income families would have a different lifestyle as evidenced in how they spent their income as compared to single-income families. While small differences were apparent, the overall pattern was that two-income and single-income families spent their income in roughly the same manner both in 1923 and in 1977. The perception of the two-income family having a bigger home, a newer automobile, more consumer goods, and taking more exotic vacations appears to be a myth. The wife's income that is left after work-related expenses seems to be added to the family income and spent on the same items as the husband's income is.

There simply was no evidence of a different lifestyle for two- versus single-income families in 1923 or in 1977.

The drastic effects of a working wife on family life and life in general that have been predicted by contemporary social commentators did not appear in the contemporary data collected in Middletown. As mentioned earlier, the Lynds did not obtain information concerning this topic, so conclusions about the effects of a working wife in 1920 remain speculation. But in 1977 working wives and housewives were equally satisfied, happy, and adjusted. There was a tendency for the husband of a working wife to be less satisfied than the husband of a housewife, but the difference was quite small.

All things considered, it seems that a working wife has a very modest effect on life satisfaction, at least as perceived by husbands and wives. These findings are reasonably consistent with other studies and indicate that the strong concern voiced about the impacts of married women working outside the home is unfounded. Perhaps one reason the effects of wives' working have been so small is that the process of married women moving into the labor force commenced nearly 80 years ago and the family and related social institutions have adjusted.

Notes

1. Edward E. Scharff, "The Two-Paycheck Life: A Subtle Revolution," *Money* 8 (no. 1) (1979):34-39.

2. James D. Wright, "Are Working Women Really More Satisfied? Evidence from Several National Surveys," *Journal of Marriage and the Family* 40 (1978):301.

3. C. Bird, *The Two-Paycheck Marriage* (New York: Rawson, Wade, 1979).

4. Robert S. Lynd and Helen M. Lynd, *Middletown* (New York: Harcourt, Brace and World, 1929).

5. Ibid., p. 26.

6. Ibid., p. 25.

7. Ibid., p. 26.

8. Ronald J. Burke and Tamara Weir, "Relationship of Wives' Employment Status to Husband, Wife and Pair Satisfaction and Performance," *Journal of Marriage and the Family* 38 (1976):279-287.

9. Ibid.

10. Myra M. Ferree, "The Confused American Housewife," *Psychology Today* 10 (1976):76-80; Myra M. Ferree, "Working Class Jobs: Housework and Paid Work as Sources of Satisfaction," *Social Problems* 23 (1976):431-441.

11. Ferree, "Working Class Jobs: Housework and Paid Work as Sources of Satisfaction."

12. Ibid., p. 440.

13. Susan R. Orden and Norman M. Bradburn, "Working Wives and Marital Happiness," *American Journal of Sociology* 74 (1969):392-407; Stephen J. Bahr and Randal Day, "Sex Role Attitudes, Female Employment and Marital Satisfaction," *Journal of Comparative Family Studies* 9 (1978):53-67.

14. Angus Campbell, "Women at Home and at Work," in *New Research on Women and Sex Roles*, ed. Dorothy G. McGuigan (Ann Arbor, Mich.: University of Michigan, 1976).

15. Wright, "Are Working Women More Satisfied."

16. Leland Axelson, "The Working Wife: Difference in Perception among Negro and White Males," *Journal of Marriage and the Family* 32 (1970):457-464.

17. Burke and Weir, "Relationship of Wives' Employment Status to Husband, Wife and Pair Satisfaction and Performance."

18. Campbell, "Women at Home and at Work."

19. Orden and Bradburn, "Working Wives and Marital Happiness."

4 The Economics of Domestic Garment-Making

Robert G. Steadman

As a producing unit, today the family is less important than it was in the preindustrial era. Civilization has evolved from a subsistence economy through a cottage trade, in which the home was also the factory, to a mass-production economy based on education and specialization. However, certain types of goods are still occasionally produced in the home, clothing being one common example. This chapter examines the efficiency of home sewing for the family's own use. The costs of making garments by the alternative methods (domestic and industrial) will be analyzed, and some peripheral economic issues will be considered such as costs and benefits in garment alterations, specialty garments, and training.

There are certain economic advantages in do-it-yourself work, advantages that are heavily promoted by those who supply the materials and tools for home industries. For instance, home vegetable growing sometimes provides a fresher, more nutritious article but at some cost. Home automobile-maintenance jobs avoid two trips to a workshop. Home wine making legally avoids federal and state excise taxes. Meal preparation using semiprepared foods is usually cheaper than "eating out." Washing and drying clothes in the home is generally more economical than the alternatives. Since labor costs associated with domestic industries are not counted in the Gross National Product, the economic importance of homemakers is commonly underestimated, and the living standards of agrarian societies are generally better than official statistics would indicate. Various noneconomic advantages such as convenience, personal satisfaction, prestige, and fashion pressures are often important in home industries but are beyond the scope of this discussion.

The supply of materials and tools to home industries is a major industry in itself since many of the materials are sold at full retail price, and the tools generally have a lower level of utilization than in commercial manufacture. This supply industry thrives on the fact that there are many more homes than factories and that materials are often bought long before they are fabricated and sometimes are never fabricated. The key to inducing people to part with their money is to persuade them that by spending now, they will somehow save at some future time.

As recently as 150 years ago, virtually all garment-making was done in the home or, for the well-to-do, by a dressmaker or tailor. Since home sewing was done by the poor majority, it has traditionally been seen as a means of saving money, even at a time when the foundation for this belief no longer exists. The belief has been cultivated by many teachers and extension agents as well as by those who sell sewing machines, fabrics, patterns, and other materials. The corresponding trade group, The National Home Sewing Association, coordinates much of this promotion.

Of the 43 textile end uses identified by the Textile Economics Bureau, the consumption of 39 fell during the recession of 1974-1975, based on a comparison of 1973 and 1975 data.[1] Of the 4 that increased, the highest rise was in retail piecegoods, strongly suggesting that many people see home garment-making as a hedge against economic adversity. During the last seven years, piecegoods have shown an averge compound annual increase of 2.4 percent by weight compared with a decrease of 0.5 percent for locally produced apparel and an increase of 0.7 percent for all textiles.[2]

In 1978, the most recent year for which full consumption data are available, the Textile Economics Bureau reported that 5,047 million pounds of textiles were produced in the United States for apparel. Of this, 450 million pounds, or about 9 percent, were retail piecegoods. Since approximately 784 million pounds of apparel, and smaller amounts of piecegoods, were imported, the proportion, in consumption, is close to 8 percent.[3] That is, if all these piecegoods were made into apparel, then about 8 percent of all the men's, women's, and children's clothes, including outerwear, underwear, knitwear, hosiery, and specialty garments were made in the home. Since common observation suggests that the proportion is below 8 percent, it appears that home sewing is associated not only with savings but with considerable waste. Precise surveys on the proportion of apparel in use that has been made in the home have yet to be made.

Since some household textiles such as sheets, blankets, towels, draperies, and upholstery could arguably be fabricated (that is, converted to a finished article) in the home, a fairer comparison may be to include these with apparel to form a category of home-sewable articles. On this basis, approximately 6 percent of sewing is done in the home, or a ratio of domestic to factory production of about 1:15.[4] If all other textiles, notably industrial textiles and carpets were included, the ratio would be 1:23. This last ratio is little more than a mathematical abstraction since the other articles do not lend themselves to home sewing.

Another statistic of interest is the apparent consumption of sewing thread. The most recent official data show 44 million pounds, or 1 pound per U.S. family, for home use, and 276 million pounds for the garment industry. Another 64 million pounds of unfinished thread of unknown destination was probably for industrial use.[5] Thus at least 11 percent of sewing thread went into home sewing. This usage may be more efficient than first impressions suggest since the home sewer with a large stock of thread in different (that is, 40 or more) shades can perform economical alterations and repairs.

Home sewing is commonly advocated as a means of reducing materials cost since the costs of manufacturing, transporting, and retailing the garment are avoided. Tacitly overlooked is the fact that these costs apply, even more severely to retail piecegoods while the commercial jobber or manufacturer buys at wholesale. If this point needs any further elaboration, one need only visit a store that sells both sheeting and sheets. The comparison of table 4-1 was based on regular prices at K-Mart and is believed to be a fair one, though it assumes that the size of a sheet is convenient to the sewer. The fact that it is over 40 percent cheaper to buy an article that has already been cut and sewn before cutting and sewing it again should be cause for some thought on the comparative economics of industrial and domestic garment-making, to which the rest of this paper will be devoted.

A recent 30-minute program on public television was devoted to home garment-making and claimed to demonstrate how a $600 dress could be made for $100. Leaving aside the question of whether public funds should be directed to that segment of the population that consumes $600 dresses, attention will be paid to two assumptions that were implicit in the program: (1) The only costs of making a garment are the costs of materials and patterns. (2) The home sewer can make a garment of quality equal to or greater than that of the commercial product.

Some remarks on the utilization and costs of materials have already been made. The same approach will be taken to the fixed costs of garment-making, using the same criteria for both types of garment manufacture. Official statistics, summarized for the most recent year, are shown and analyzed in table 4-2. A striking feature is that more than seven times as many domestic as industrial sewing machines are purchased annually. Most of the industrial machines are American-made while 99 percent of domestic sewing machines are imported. The import duty of 5 percent is well below the

Table 4-1
Retail Costs of Two Forms of Cloth

| | Polyester/Cotton Printed Percale, Thread Count 156 | |
	As Piecegoods	As Made-up Sheets
Size	1 yd. × 45 in.	97 in. × 82 in. + hems (flat double-bed sheet)
Price	$2.27 per yard	$6.57
Price per square yard	$1.83	$1.07

Note: Prices obtained from K-Mart in Colorado during 1979.

Table 4-2
Comparison of Major Components in Garment-Making

U.S. Production and Imports Less Exports	Domestic	Factory	Ratio, Domestic: Factory
Textile fibers (million pounds)[a]	450	4,597 (for apparel)	1:10
		5,879 (for home-sewable articles)	1:13
		11,619 (total)	1:26
Sewing thread (million dollars)[a]	44	276 (+64?)	1:6 or 8
Sewing machines (number)	1,677,000	233,000	7:1
(Million dollars wholesale)	155	126	5:4 (wholesale) 2:1 (as purchased)
Average cost per machine, retail	190	540	1:3
Machine utilization (pounds of home-sewable articles per machine sold)	268	25,232	1:94

Source: The Textile Economics Bureau. *Textile Organon*, 50 (November 1979):174-176.

[a]U.S. production for U.S. use only. For both domestic and factory production, net imports of textile products are less than 15 percent by weight of U.S. consumption.

approximately 30 percent levied on imported apparel and would seem to offer an advantage to those who make their own clothes. Given the appreciable retail mark-up, we conclude that approximately twice as much is spent on domestic as on industrial machines, despite their lower total output, previously shown as in the ratio 1:15.

It follows that the output of the average industrial machine exceeds that of the average domestic machine by a factor of 93, despite a cost nearly three times higher (see table 4-2). Interestingly, the most expensive machines, at prices approaching $1,000, are domestic models. There are approximately 1.2 million industrial machines in place. If we assume that a domestic machine lasts twice as long as its cousin in the factory, we conclude that about 17 million domestic machines are in American homes. This very rough figure is not used in table 4-2, which is based on the more exact data on annual sales. The ratio of 93 underestimates the true utilization ratio since it overlooks the nonusage of some materials, especially in the home; and it does not include the sewing of industrial products such as auto interiors but does include the industrial machines needed to do this.

With this information from table 4-2, the chief overhead costs can be analyzed. If factories convert 5,879 million pounds of home-sewable articles with 1.2 million machines, each machine processes 490 pounds annually. Since annual purchases are 233,000 (1/5 of 1.2 million), a depreciation allowance of 20 percent is reasonable. Since fabric typically yields 4 yards per pound, annual machine costs with a $540 machine is about 5 1/2 cents per yard [($540 × 0.20)/(490 pounds × 4 yards/pound) = $.055/yard]. For the domestic machine, with lower cost and utilization and a depreciation rate of only 10 percent, cost per yard is about 83 cents ($.05 × 25232/268 × 190/540 × 10/20 = $.828; the utilization ratios are taken from table 4-2).

Cloth cutting costs are less readily analyzed but also seem to favor the industrial sewer. The factory cutter is typically a skilled male using an electric knife on 100 to 120 fabric layers simultaneously. Domestic equipment, a cutting board and scissors, is simple but requires considerable floor space relative to output.

Although some home sewers can function in a closet, a more reasonable comparison of floor space is shown in table 4-3. Similar calculations, based on 5-percent tax and depreciation for both domestic and industrial floor space, give a cost per yard of 5 cents for industrial and $1.97 for domestic manufacture.

In making clothes in the home, the homemaker is competing with a low-wage industry. Average hourly wages in the U.S. apparel industry are now only $4.15 for a 35-hour week.[6] This is the lowest of all manufacturing industries, and there are few places where so little is paid for so much skill. Moreover, garments are imported from countries where hourly wages are well below $1. The U.S. industry has a high turnover rate with considerable training costs, typically 5 to 10 percent of the costs of operation. Corresponding costs to the domestic sewer are comparable (see table 4-4). This calculation assumes a person taking three courses at a state university (construction, tailoring, and flat pattern). In industry, six weeks of totally lost production at $3.00 per hour plus payroll taxes, with a 25-percent government training subsidy, are assumed. The trainee, unlike the student, receives wages, and thus has no time cost. Both total training costs are comparable but, because of the industrial operator's full-time production, her per-garment cost will be much lower.

One-of-a-Kind Garments

Theatrical costume comes to mind as an example of a good that does not lend itself to mass production. In some high schools, production for school plays is an appreciable part of garment-construction courses. Here the home sewer may have an advantage in the direct, if not the fixed costs, of making a garment.

This leads to the less quantifiable question of making an exclusive fashion article that will be seen on nobody else at a gathering. Many conditions must

Table 4-3
Comparative Practices and Costs of Garment Manufacturing

	Apparel Industry	Home Manufacture
Pattern utilization: Garments typically made per pattern	Dozens (high fashion, unit price) Hundreds (low fashion, dozen price) Thousands (with grading)	0 or 1 Limited facilities for grading
Cutting: Fabrics cut simultaneously	100	1 or 2
Garments cut simultaneously	50	1
Typical sewing-machine speed (stitches per minute)	5,000 to 8,000	Variable to 1500
Cost of sewing machine	$80 to $800, average $540	$400 to $800, average $190
Floor space per machine	100 sq. ft. @ $20	30 sq. ft. @ $30
Cost of unused materials	Low, but appreciable in high-fashion manufacture	Apparently very high
Direct costs per square yard of fabric:		
Fabric	0.60	1.83 (retail piecegoods) 1.07 (cut from sheets)
Lining, thread, and other materials at 50%	0.30	0.53
Machine maintenance and repair	0.04	0.04
Cutting (approx.)	0.20	0.20
Wages or opportunity cost of time, assumed equal, for sewing operations	0.55	0.55
Total of above direct costs	1.69	2.39
Fixed (indirect) costs per square yard:		
Sewing machine depreciation	0.05	0.82
Floor space @ 5%	0.05	1.97
Administration other than training	0.30	0.00
Total of above indirect costs	.40	2.79
Total of above costs	2.09	5.18
Pattern cost per garment	0.25	2.50 (half price)
Training cost per garment	0.76	5.40
Manufacturing cost of 5 sq. yd. garment	11.46	34.99[a]
Distribution costs: Transport at 15%	1.72	0.00
Subtotal	13.28	34.99
Retail mark-up @ 36% (average)	4.78	0.00
Total cost of garment	18.06	34.99

[a]Using cheapest option, includes $1.19 for waste when 45-sq. ft. garment is cut from 55 sq. ft. sheet—.

Table 4-4
Costs and Benefits of Alternative Training Methods for Garment-Making

		For Apparel Industry	*For Home Manufacture*
Training cost:	To individual	$ 0	$ 270 + Time
	To taxpayer	190	810
	To company	570	0
	Total	$ 760	$1,080 + Time
Benefits at end of training period:			
	Skill	High	High
	Productivity	High	Medium
	Versatility	Low	High
Guesstimated number of garments made during career after this training		1,000	200
Training cost per garment		0.76	5.40

be met before the direct costs are comparable with those of a garment bought at retail: well-selected materials and the time and skill to make a garment that looks handmade rather than homemade; even then it will not carry an exclusive designer label that can be casually displayed each time the garment is draped on a chair or laid on a bed. When fixed costs are taken into account, the cheapest way of getting the desired garment may well be to pay full retail price for the finished article.

Alterations

The conversion of out-of-fashion garments into attractive contemporary fashion goods enhances their commercial value greatly and is sometimes a remunerative adjunct of dry-cleaning plants. To the individual, the ability to adjust children's garments to their growth may be of personal, if not commercial value. For a home sewer with some skill and even simple equipment, alterations may give a return comparable with that of the minimum wage—and tax free!

Alternatives

Clearly, domestic garment-making must be done on a large scale—larger than the averge family could consume—to be economically justifiable. The practice of advising an untrained, low-income woman that she can save money by investing in a sewing machine and the various other supplies needed to make garments is a cruel hoax that benefits only the suppliers. What sort of advice *can* be given to help people reduce the 7 percent of family income spent on apparel?

Now that man-made fibers account for 75 percent of our fiber consumption, durability has increased. The four-year cotton bedsheet has been superseded by the polyester/cotton sheet that lasts ten years. Thus an increasing proportion of garments may be discarded before being truly worn out. The media of exchange, garage sales, 50-50 stores, and charities deserve attention, and more people could be directed to them. Such purchases, combined with judicious alterations, may provide substantial savings without the investments of money and time needed to make a garment from scratch. For example, I purchased a good parka for one dollar at a garage sale, and it has given me several years of service. Stewart has identified various outlets of used apparel for women.[7]

More defensively, ready-to-wear apparel represents good value. With the consumer price index at 216, the apparel index is 154, that is, apparel prices have increased at less than half the rate of the overall cost of living.[8]

Perhaps a relevant comment is that of Sweeney and Thompson in 1965: that the reasons for home sewing are factors such as "enjoyment . . . There appeared to be no economic pressure."[9] But this misses the point that economic costs typically exceed economic benefits. Further, time spent on home-manufacturing tasks requiring individual skill and concentration is time that is not available for family interaction. I suggest that any claims of "savings" in home sewing undergo objective economic analysis before any investment is made.

Notes

1. Textile Economics Bureau, *Textile Organon* 48 (November 1977):174.

2. Textile Economics Bureau, *Textile Organon* 50 (November 1979):174-176.

3. Ibid., p. 182.

4. These figures were computed from data reported in *Textile Organon* 50 (no. 11) (1979):182. There were 5,831 million pounds of textiles available for apparel plus about 1,130 million pounds in sheets, blankets, towels, drapes, and upholstery, for a total of about 6,961 million pounds. The 450 million pounds of retail piecegoods divided by 6,961 equals 6.46 percent, or a ratio of about 1:15.

5. U.S. Bureau of the Census, *Annual Survey of Manufactures, 1973*, M73 (AS-1) (Washington, D.C.: Government Printing Office, 1975).

6. American Textile Manufacturers Institute, *Textile Highlights*, December 1978.

7. S.L. Stewart, "Outlets Offering Used Apparel for Women," (M.S. Thesis, Colorado State University, 1968).

8. U.S. Bureau of the Census, *Statistical Abstract of the United States: 1978*, 99th ed. (Washington, D.C.: Government Printing Office, 1978).

9. Beverly S. Sweeney and Henrietta M. Thompson, "Sewing Practices of Mothers of Pre-school Children," *Journal of Home Economics* 57 (1965):660-661.

**Part II
The Economics of
Fertility**

5 A Stock Adjustment Model of Child-Spacing and Desired Family Size

Hyman Joseph

Introduction

Couples' fertility decisions can be thought of as including a decision about desired completed family size as well as a decision about child-spacing. These two decisions would usually be made simultaneously and would be subject to modifications over time as new information is gathered. The implementation of these decisions would be subject to random or stochastic elements that might frustrate or modify the realization of these decisions. This chapter incorporates all the preceeding parts of the decision-making process into a formal model (a stock adjustment model) and provides empirical estimates of that model by utilizing the data of the 1965 National Fertility Study (NFS). In addition, this chapter provides estimates of the net effect of each of several interesting variables on the realized fertility of the respondents in the 1965 NFS.

The next section of this chapter, "The Model," develops the stock adjustment model and from it an equation that is suitable for empirical estimation and testing. The section after that, "Empirical Estimation," presents the empirical results. Those readers who are not interested in the formal model (or who are very impatient) may proceed directly to this section. The final section provides a summary and conclusions.

The Model

The family-size decision process is hypothesized to be as follows. A couple compares the number of children that it desires with the number of children it has and decides on a spacing strategy. The spacing strategy could be, for example, to have one child every three years. The decisions are reviewed periodically and may be revised as circumstances change. The preceding type of decision process is called a "stock adjustment model." This type of model has been used widely to explain business investment in plant and equipment[1] and has been applied to aggregate fertility behavior.[2]

This research was financed by Public Health Service Grant No. 5R01HD07818, which was awarded by the National Institute of Child Health and Human Development.

In a general form, the desired number of children (or the desired completed family size) at some point of time t, C_t^*, can be expressed as a function of several variables denoted by the letter X.

$$C_t^* = f(X_1, X_2, \cdots, X_K) \tag{5.1}$$

The number of additional children desired for the next year, N_t^*, can be expressed as a function of the difference between the desired number of children and the actual number of children, C_t.

$$N_t^* = g(C_t^* - C_t) \tag{5.2}$$

The symbol g could represent some parameter (or number), or it could be a function of other variables such as the following:

$$g = h(S_1, S_2, \cdots, S_j) \tag{5.3}$$

The actual number of additional children for the next year, N_t, would equal the desired number plus an error term.

$$N_t = N_t^* + u_t \tag{5.4}$$

Equations 5.1 through 5.4 describe how N_t is determined in this stock adjustment model. The main determinants of N_t are the X variables that affect the desired number of chilren, the S variables that affect the desired child-spacing, the stochastic error u_t, and the functional forms of equations 5.1 through 5.4.

To estimate a stock adjustment model empirically, a more specific formulation is required with respect to choosing the X and S variables, the selection of appropriate functional forms, and the selection of appropriate error structures. The following is such a specification. One convenient form for equation 5.1 is a linear one.

$$C_t^* = b_0 + b_1 X_1 + \cdots + b_K X_K \tag{5.5}$$

A reasonable specification for equation 5.3 might be one in which the proportion of the gap between C_t^* and C_t that is desired to be closed in the next year depends on the spacing variables relative to the size of the gap, $C_t^* - C_t$.

$$g = \frac{a_0 + a_1 S_1 + a_2 S_2 + \cdots + a_j S_j}{C_t^* - C_t} \tag{5.6}$$

When that gap is zero, then g is not defined in equation 5.6. This presents no problems since when the gap is zero, the proportion of the gap that is desired to be closed is not defined conceptually and is therefore of no interest. If equations 5.2, 5.5, and 5.6 are substituted into equation 5.4, then equation 5.7 is obtained.

$$N_t = a_0 b_0 + a_1 S_1 + a_2 S_2 + \cdots + a_j S_j + a_0 b_1 X_1 + \cdots$$
$$+ a_0 b_K X_K - a_0 C_t + u_t \tag{5.7}$$

The coefficients of equation 5.7 can be estimated empirically. Estimates of the coefficients of equations 5.5 and 5.6 then can be obtained by appropriate transformations of the estimated coefficients of equation 5.7.

The preceding is one of many possible specifications of the functional forms of the stock adjustment model. This specification is relatively easy to estimate empirically and a priori appears to be a reasonable one.

Empirical Estimation

The data to be utilized are from the 1965 National Fertility (NFS).[3] The coded responses to the interview questions are transformed to form mostly dichotomous variables (that take on the value either zero or unity) and a few quantitative variables. The transformed variables are used to represent the variables in equation 5.7. Some of the transformed variables are designated as X variables, which affect the desired number of children, and some are designated as S variables, which affect child-spacing. The dependent variable, N_t, is a dichotomous one and takes on the value unity if a live birth occurred in the previous 12 months and zero otherwise.

The variables that are hypothesized to affect child-spacing include the fecundity of the respondent (R), R's age, contraception ever used, and R's work status. The variables that are hypothesized to affect desired number of children include size of place of residence, years of schooling (R), years of schooling of husband (H), H's 1965 income, R's 1965 income, R's race, number of babies born alive to R's mother, R's religious preference, and H's religious preference. The reasons for the inclusion of the preceding variables and their hypothesized effect on the dependent variable will be discussed in conjunction with the following presentation of the empirical results. Some variables that were considered in the preliminary analyses and were found not to be statistically significant are not included in this paper.[4] These variables include: schooling of R's father, schooling of R's mother, schooling of H's father, and schooling of H's mother.

Both ordinary least squares (OLS) and generalized least squares (GLS) are utilized to estimate equation 5.7. GLS is utilized because heteroscedasticity may be present when the dependent variable is dichotomous, and this estimation procedure produces more efficient estimates of the standard errors of the estimated coefficients.[5] However, GLS increases the problem of multicollinearity because each variable in the estimating equation is multiplied by the same variable (as explained in footnote 5). Since neither OLS or GLS is dominant, both are utilized.

Table 5-1 presents the empirical results for five models (versions of equation 5.7) that differ by the variables that are included, the ways in which the variables are grouped, and/or the method of estimation. Model 1 has the largest number of variables and is estimated by OLS. Model 2 has the identical set of variables but is estimated by GLS. Models 3, 4, and 5 are estimated by OLS. Model 3 has fewer variables than Model 1 (or 2) and differs mainly in that some categories of variables have been transformed. For example, size of place of residence and husband's 1965 income have broader categories. Model 4 has some variables categorized like model 1 (or 2) and some like model 3. Model 5 utilizes the variable Ideal Number of Children (R) in lieu of the variables that represent desired number of children in the four other models. The purpose of estimating model 5 is to see how the response to a direct question regarding desired number of children compares to inferring the desired number from other variables for the purpose of predicting actual behavior (represented by the dependent variable).

The hypothesized sign for the number-of-previous-children variable is negative since more children would mean that the couple was closer to its desired number and therefore less likely to have more children. The estimated coefficients are negative in all five models and statistically significant at the 1-percent level in models 1 through 4.

The fecundity variables are presumed to affect child-spacing. They are dummy variables that take on the value unity or zero. If the respondent is classified as sterile, then both the fecund and the subfecund variable take on the value zero. As expected, fecund respondents were more likely to have births than sterile respondents, and the estimated coefficients of the fecund variable are statistically significant at the 1-percent level in all five models. No statistically significant difference was found between those classified as subfecund and those classified as sterile.

The variable contraception ever used is a zero-one dummy variable. It was included to check if those who were amendable to using contraception had different child-spacing than those who were not. The estimated coefficient of this variable is positive in both of the models in which it is used and is statistically significant at the 1-percent level in model 2. An explanation of this result is that those respondents who were amendable to using con-

Table 5-1
1965 National Fertility-Study Regression Results, Dependent Variable: Live Birth in Last 12 Months, Yes or No
(Standard Errors in parentheses)

Independent Variable or Statistic (Standard Case in Parentheses)	Model				
	1	2 (GLS)	3	4	5
Constant	$-.0889^a$	$-.4955^b$	$-.0697$	$-.0755^a$	$-.1519^b$
	(.0450)	(.0633)	(.0352)	(.0351)	(.0185)
Number of previous children	$-.0094^b$	$-.0169^b$	$-.00865^b$	$-.00877^b$	$-.0041$
	(.0023)	(.0017)	(.00221)	(.00221)	(.0021)
Fecundity (sterile) Subfecund	$-.0115$	$-.0090$	$-.0133$	$-.0135$	$-.0100$
	(.0135)	(.0083)	(.0133)	(.0134)	(.0133)
Fecund	$.0389^b$	$.0831^b$	$.0430^b$	$.0432^b$	$.0376^b$
	(.0120)	(.0088)	(.0116)	(.0117)	(.0116)
Contraception ever used	$.0194$	$.0322^b$			
	(.0119)	(.0081)			
R's date of birth (century months ÷ 100)	$.0699^b$	$.1248^b$	$.0716^b$	$.0714^b$	$.0764^b$
	(.0047)	(.0079)	(.0046)	(.0046)	(.0045)
Size of place of residence (Rural farm)					
A. Central cities	$-.0420^a$	$-.1022^b$			
	(.0207)	(.0133)			
B. Cities 150,000 or more	$-.0390^a$	$-.0805^b$			
	(.0199)	(.0135)			
C. Cities 50,000-149,999	$-.0246$	$-.0545^b$			
	(.0219)	(.0140)			
D. Rings of 14 largest cities	$-.0496^a$	$-.1082^b$			
	(.0197)	(.0136)			
E. Rings of other cities	$-.0426^a$	$-.0869^b$			
	(.0178)	(.0112)			
F. Cities 25,000-49,999	$-.0325$	$-.0645^b$			
	(.0184)	(.0108)			
G. Rural nonfarm	$-.0253$	$-.0498^b$			
	(.0185)	(.0123)			
$A + B + D + E$			$-.0398^a$	$-.0414^a$	
			(.0161)	(.0162)	
$C + F + G$			$-.0253$	$-.0275$	
			(.0162)	(.0162)	
Region of residence (Far West)					
A. Northeast	$-.0222$	$-.0452^b$			$-.0203$
	(.0151)	(.0104)			(.0145)
B. Midwest	$-.0318^a$	$-.0641^b$	$-.0340^a$		$-.0317^a$
	(.0141)	(.0101)	(.0140)		(.0137)
C. South	$-.0198$	$-.0378^b$			$-.0186$
	(.0143)	(.0092)			(.0138)
$A + C$			$-.0216$		
			(.0123)		

Table 5-1 *(continued)*

Independent Variable or Statistic (Standard Case in Parentheses	Model				
	1	*2 (GLS)*	*3*	*4*	*5*
Years of schooling (*R*)	−.0014 (.0023)	−.0063[b] (.0014)			
Years of schooling (*H*)	.0023 (.0018)	.0025 (.0013)			
Husband's 1965 income					
($15,000 or more)					
Under $2,000	.0571 (.0312)	.0328[a] (.0167)	.0496 (.0298)	.0453 (.0298)	
$2,000-$2,999	.0750[b] (.0293)	.0678[b] (.0192)		.0643[a] (.0276)	
$3,000-$3,999	.0796[b] (.0265)	.0838[b] (.0144)		.0698[b] (.0250)	
$4,000-$4,999	.0384 (.0250)	.0213 (.0143)		.0305 (.0237)	
$5,000-$5,999	.0245 (.0236)	−.0024 (.0134)		.0196 (.0224)	
$6,000-$6,999	.0309 (.0238)	.0207 (.0146)		.0268 (.0223)	
$7,000-$7,999	.0494[a] (.0246)	.0510[b] (.0145)		.0456 (.0239)	
$8,000-$8,999	.0532[a] (.0259)	.0597[b] (.0169)		.0497[a] (.0253)	
$9,000-$9,999	.0057 (.0275)	−.0230 (.0181)		.0052 (.0271)	
$10,000-$11,999	.0168 (.0252)	.0157 (.0157)		.0163 (.0249)	
$12,000-$14,999	.0317 (.0272)	.0325 (.0168)	.0325 (.0272)	.0307 (.0272)	
$2,000-$3,999			.0706[b] (.0237)		
$4,000-$5,999			.0257 (.0218)		
$6,000-$8,999			.0391 (.0213)		
$9,000-$11,999			.0114 (.0230)		
Respondent's 1965 income					
(No income)					
Under $2,000	−.0451[b] (.0157)	−.0842[b] (.0114)			
$2,000-$2,999	−.0509[a] (.0212)	−.0821[b] (.0157)		−.0187 (.0179)	
$3,000-$3,999	−.0327 (.0221)	−.0489[b] (.0151)		.0004 (.0188)	

Table 5-1 *(continued)*

Independent Variable or Statistic (Standard Case in Parentheses	Model				
	1	*2 (GLS)*	*3*	*4*	*5*
$4,000-$4,999	− .0513[a]	− .0711[b]		− .0186	
	(.0244)	(.0177)		(.0213)	
$5,000-$5,999	− .0691[a]	− .1327[b]		− .0326	
	(.0296)	(.0189)		(.0268)	
$6,000-$6,999	− .0205	− .0072		.0130	
	(.0389)	(.0251)		(.0366)	
$7,000 +	− .0202	− .0329		.0129	
	(.0421)	(.0245)		(.0400)	
Under $3,000			− .0453[b]		
			(.0151)		
$3,000-$5,999			− .0441[a]		
			(.0188)		
$6,000 +			− .0189		
			(.0304)		
R's working status— working	− .0495[b]	− .0980[b]	− .0509[b]	− .0794[b]	− .0797[b]
	(.0162)	(.0111)	(.0159)	(.0123)	(.0089)
R's race (black)					
Other nonwhite	.0097	− .0174			
	(.0392)	(.0405)			
White	− .0641[b]	− .1230[b]	− .0620[b]	− .0600[b]	
	(.0131)	(.0109)	(.0117)	(.0118)	
Number of babies born alive to R's mother	.0028[a]	.0029[b]	.00272[a]	.00285[a]	
	(.0014)	(.0009)	(.00133)	(.00133)	
R's religious preference (Protestant)					
Roman Catholic	.0236	.0322[b]	.0283	.0407[b]	
	(.0156)	(.0120)	(.0200)	(.0105)	
Jewish	.0575	.1023	− .0140		
	(.0775)	(.0675)	(.0332)		
Nothing or no answer	.0296	.0428	.0416		
	(.0465)	(.0378)	(.0436)		
Other	− .0271	− .0194	− .0061		
	(.0410)	(.0335)	(.0275)		
H's religious preference (Protestant)					
Roman Catholic	.0254	.0610[b]			
	(.0159)	(.0124)			
Jewish	− .0791	− .1340[a]			
	(.0774)	(.0668)			
Nothing or no answer	.0209	.0400[a]			
	(.0236)	(.0164)			
Other	.0299	.0312			
	(.0454)	(.0347)			
Both R and H Roman Catholic			.0139		
			(.0215)		

Table 5-1 *(continued)*

Independent Variable or Statistic (Standard Case in Parentheses	Model				
	1	*2 (GLS)*	*3*	*4*	*5*
Ideal number of children (*R*)					.00081
					(.00049)
R Square	.136	.088	.134	.133	.117
Number of observations	5172	4237	5172	5172	5174

[a]Statistically significant at the 5-percent probability level.
[b]Statistically significant at the 1-percent probability level.

traception were more likely to give birth in 1965. This may be a variable that is affected by the business cycle, and different results might be obtained in recession years.

The respondent's date of birth (in century months divided by 100) is presumed to be a child-spacing variable that affects fecundity. Higher birth dates (which mean younger ages) should be associated with higher likelihood of birth so that a positive coefficient is hypothesized. All five models have positive coefficients that are statistically significant at the 1-percent level.

The final child-spacing variables are dummy variables that relate to *R*'s work status. It is hypothesized that respondents who are working are less likely to desire a birth in the current year than those who are not working. Also those respondents who had a birth in the previous 12 months may be less likely to be working at the time of the survey. The estimated coefficient has the hypothesized negative sign in all five models and is statistically significant at the 1-percent level.

The size of place of residence is represented by a set of dummy variables. When all the variables are set equal to zero, then the respondent lives on a farm. It is hypothesized that the desired number of children would be smaller in more congested places where the costs of children would be larger. The estimated coefficients of all of the size of place of residence variables are negative. The respondents who live in the more congested places are less likely to have births than respondents who live on farms, and several of those estimated coefficients are statistically significant at the 1- or 5-percent level. Models 3 and 4 aggregate the size of place of residence variables into only two dummy variables. That aggregation is based on the regression results from models 1 and 2. In summary, the results indicate that respondents in more congested places of residence are less likely to have births.

The region of residence variables are included because costs of children may differ among regions. Housing and fuel costs would generally be higher in the Midwest and Northeast than in the South and Far West (represented by all zeros for the dummy variables). The likelihood of a birth in the midwest region is found to be lower than in the far west region. The likelihoods of a birth in the Northeast or South are between the likelihoods for the Far West and Midwest.

Education variables are often included in fertility studies. Education could affect a couple's preference for children versus commodities, or it could affect contraceptive knowledge, or it could be a proxy for other variables such as income. In this study the proxy effect is eliminated because income variables are included. Years of schooling of the respondent is shown to have a negative effect on fertility while years of schooling of the husband has a positive but not statistically significant effect.

Income can affect the desired number of children in two ways. First, higher income allows a couple to buy more commodities for itself and for existing or prospective children. A couple could then "afford" to have more children and/or commodities. But a couple could increase only its purchase of commodities or only its desired number of children, or it could even decide to reduce desired consumption of either commodities or children to enable it to increase the consumption of the one not reduced even more. Second, higher income increases the costs of children since most children are raised with a standard of living similar to that of their parents.[6] So the effect of higher income on the desired number of children, and therefore on actual births, is not predictable from theoretical considerations only. Empirical observations are required.

The 1965 NFS has data on husband's 1965 income (before taxes) and respondent's 1965 income (before taxes). Ideally, we would like information on expected future or permanent income since family-size decisions may be based on such an income concept. However, since such data are not available, actual income is used instead. Consequently, some bias may occur in the estimation of the regression coefficients.

The effect of husband's 1965 income (before taxes) on the likelihood of a birth is not monotonic. The coefficient of each income class variable contrasts the effect of that class with the $15,000-and-over class. As we move from the lowest income class to higher classes, the coefficients first increase to a maximum at the $3,000-$3,999 class and then diminish and then rise to a relative maximum at the $8,000-$8,999 class. These results are, of course, consistent with the earlier theoretical discussion. Virtually any results would be. But the important point is that the effect of income on births is not monotonic because higher income can raise the cost of children as well as allowing the family to purchase more commodities.

The effect of respondents' 1965 income (before taxes) on the likelihood of a birth is also not monotonic. The coefficient of each income class variable contrasts the effect of that class with the no income (not working) class for models 1, 2, and 3, and the no income or under $2,000 class for model 4. The peak negative effect of respondents' income on fertility appears in the $5,000-$5,999 income class.

The coefficients of the variables for race of respondent show a lower likelihood of births for white respondents than for black respondents (represented by all zeros for the dummy variables), and that difference is statistically significant at the 1-percent probability level. Other nonwhite respondents show no statistically significant coefficient in model 1 and 2, and are grouped with the black respondents in models 3 and 4. The observed differences in births between white respondents and other respondents are not due to income, or education, or any other variables that are included in the regression analysis and therefore are held constant. Apparently, there are differences in preferences for number of children between white respondents and nonwhite respondents.

The variable called number of babies born alive to R's mother would be positively related to desired number of children if the respondents tended to favor the type of family environment, regarding number of children, in which they grew up. This variable has an estimated positive coefficient that is statistically significant at the 5- (or 1) percent probability level in all four models in which it is included.

The religious-preference variables for the respondent are highly correlated with those for the husband since people tend to marry others with the same religious preference. This presents a statistical problem of multicollinearity, which makes it difficult to tell whether it is the religious preference of the respondent or that of the husband that affects behavior. Model 3 omits H's religious preference but includes an interaction term for both R and H Roman Catholic. Model 4 omits H's religious preference and classified respondents as Roman Catholic or all other. The omission of the husband's religious preference tends to overstate the effect of the respondent's religious preference. Overall, the results tend to show that those with Roman Catholic religious preferences are more likely to have births. Statistically significant coefficients (1-percent probability level) were obtained in models 2 and 4.

In model 5 the variable ideal number of children (R), which was obtained from a question in the NFS, is utilized to represent desired number of children in lieu of the other variables that are in models 1 through 4. This variable was not statistically significant at the 5-percent probability level and resulted in a reduction in the overall R^2 compared to the other three models (1, 3, and 4) that had the same dependent variable. (The GLS transformation of model 2 transformed the dependent variable and thereby made its R^2 not comparable to the other models.) These results suggest that this particular question elicits responses that are not adequate to infer desired number of children.

Child-Spacing Results

The earlier statement of the model posits that the proportion of the gap between C^*_t and C_t that is desired to be closed in the next year depends on the

spacing variables are specified in equation 5.6. The variable g in equation 5.6 is a function of the variables on the right-hand side of equation 5.6 and may range from zero to unity. Given the estimated coefficients from the regression models, one can construct a table relating g to hypothetical values of the spacing variables. Table 5-2 is such a table for the case where the gap between desired and actual is one child. As discussed previously, the spacing variables include age of respondent, fecundity, and work status.

The estimated child-spacings for the ranges of the variables that were selected range from 0.13 in model 4 for a subfecund, working respondent of

Table 5-2
1965 NFS Estimated Child-Spacing
(When Gap Between Desired and Actual Number of Children is Unity)

Age of Respondent	Fecund		Subfecund	
	Working	Not Working	Working	Not Working
Model 1[a]				
20	.40	.45	.35	.40
25	.35	.40	.30	.35
30	.31	.36	.26	.31
35	.27	.32	.22	.27
40	.23	.28	.18	.23
Model 2[a]				
20	.71	.81	.62	.71
25	.63	.73	.54	.64
30	.56	.66	.47	.56
35	.48	.58	.39	.49
40	.41	.51	.32	.41
Model 3				
20	.39	.43	.33	.39
25	.34	.38	.28	.34
30	.30	.34	.24	.30
35	.26	.30	.20	.26
40	.21	.25	.15	.21
Model 4				
20	.36	.44	.31	.39
25	.31	.39	.26	.34
30	.27	.35	.22	.30
35	.23	.31	.18	.26
40	.18	.26	.13	.21
Model 5				
20	.37	.45	.32	.40
25	.33	.41	.27	.36
30	.28	.36	.23	.31
35	.24	.32	.19	.27
40	.19	.27	.14	.22

[a]For respondents who had never used contraception.

age 40 to 0.81 in model 2 for a fecund, not-working respondent of age 20. The interpretation of an estimated child-spacing of say 0.40 is that 40 out of every 100 respondents who ultimately desired to have one more child had one during the year. The child-spacing estimates do not vary greatly among the four models that are estimated by OLS but are higher for model 2, which is estimated by GLS.

Child-spacings can be calculated when the gap between desired and actual number of children is, say, two children. Equation 5.6 would yield the child-spacing for two additional desired children. The child-spacing for one more desired child is found by multiplying these results by 2. Since the estimates of the constant term in equation 5.6 have positive signs in all five models, greater number of additional desired children is associated with a quicker acquisition of the next child. However, the empirical results indicate that they are not acquired much more quickly since the estimates of the constant term in equation 5.6 are not quantitatively large.

Desired Number of Children

The estimated desired number of children depends on the characteristics of the respondent such as is expressed in equation 5.5. These estimates can be derived from the regressions in the form of equation 5.7 by appropriate transformations, mainly dividing through the relevant regression estimates by minus the estimated coefficient of number of previous children. Then these estimates of coefficients represented by the letter b and various subscripts in equation 5.5 are multiplied by selected values of the X variables to obtain the estimated desired number of children. The number of different characteristics of the respondents is large, and every combination of characteristics would have a different estimated desired number of children. The estimates are volatile with respect to a change in the characteristics of a hypothetical respondent and therefore would not be useful for predicting desired number of children based on the characteristics of the respondents that were included in this study.

Summary and Conclusions

This chapter views fertility decisions of couples as including both a desired family-size decision and a child-spacing decision. Both of these parts of the fertility decision process are presumed to be made at the same time and to be subject to modifications over time as new information is gathered. A stock adjustment model provides a formal model of the fertility decision process. Empirical estimates of the parameters of the stock adjustment model are made by utilizing the data of the 1965 National Fertility Study (NFS).

The conclusions of this study are divided into two parts. First, the estimated effect of each of several variables on fertility, holding the other variables constant, is presented. These estimated effects are of interest even outside the context of a stock adjustment model. Second, the estimated patterns of child-spacing and desired family size are presented within the context of the stock adjustment model of this chapter.

The conclusions regarding the net effect of individual variables on fertility as estimated from the 1965 NFS follow.

1. Larger values for number of previous children reduced the estimated probability of a new birth.
2. Those women classified as sterile had a lower probability of having a birth than those classified as fecund. No statistically significant difference was found between those classified as sterile and those classified as subfecund.
3. Those respondents who had *ever* used contraception were found to be more likely to have a birth in 1965. The effect of this variable may depend on general economic conditions and may be different in those years where economic conditions are less favorable than in 1965.
4. Age of respondent and fertility were found to be inversely related.
5. Respondents who were employed at the time of the survey were found to have a lower probability of having a birth.
6. More congested places of residence, which would be expected to have higher costs of raising children, were found to reduce the likelihood of births.
7. The likelihood of a birth in the midwest region of the United States was found to be lower than in the far west region, while the likelihoods for the Northeast and South were between the likelihoods of the Far West and Midwest.
8. Years of schooling of the respondent was found to have a negative effect on fertility, while years of schooling of the husband had a positive but not statistically significant effect.
9. The effect of husband's 1965 income on fertility was found not to be monotonic. Two relative peaks with positive estimated coefficients were found in the intermediate income range.
10. The effect of respondent's 1965 income on fertility was also found not to be monotonic. The peak negative effect of respondent's income on fertility appeared in an intermediate income class.
11. White respondents were found to have lower fertility than black respondents.
12. The number of babies born alive to the respondent's mother was found to be positively related to fertility.
13. Those couples where the respondent and/or her husband had Roman Catholic religious preferences were found to be more likely to have a birth.

The second set of conclusions relate to child-spacing and desired family size within the context of a stock adjustment model. Child-spacing estimates depend on such variables as age of respondent, fecundity, work status, and contraception ever used. Desired family-size estimates are based on most of the other variables that were included in the regression analysis. The child-spacing results are expressed as the proportion of the couples who desired to have one more child that had one during the year. The second set of conclusions follow.

1. All the estimated child-spacings were in the 0-1 interval, which is consistent with the stock adjustment model that was utilized.
2. The child-spacing results were not sensitive to the choice of or grouping of variables that were used to estimate desired family size but were sensitive to the method of statistical estimation (OLS or GLS).
3. The child-spacing estimates showed that the greater the number of additional children that are desired, the more quickly the couple acquired their next child.
4. The estimates of desired number of children were volatile with respect to a change in the characteristics of the respondent. A variable based on a survey question regarding ideal number of children was utilized in lieu of estimating desired number of children from several characteristics of the respondent and her husband. But this alternative reduced the overall explanatory power of the regression equation.

Notes

1. For examples, see E. Greenberg, "A Stock Adjustment Investment Model," *Econometrica* 32 (1964):339-357; H.M. Hochman, "Some Aggregative Implications of Depreciation Acceleration," *Yale Economic Essays* 6 (1966):216-274; H. Joseph, "Costs of Adjustment and the Flexible Accelerator," *Western Economic Journal* 8 (1970):24-36.

2. P.R. Gregory, "A Stock Adjustment Model of Fertility: The White and Non-white U.S. Populations (1946-1970)," 1973, University of Houston, unpublished.

3. A description of this study may be found in N.B. Ryder and C.F. Westoff, *Reproduction in the United States 1965* (Princeton: Princeton University Press, 1971).

4. These variables were included in some of the analyses contained in the *Final Progress Report* of PHS grant number R01HD07818, May 1978.

5. A.S. Goldberger, *Econometric Theory* (New York: Wiley, 1964), p. 249, shows that when the dependent variable is a qualitative variable, the

classical assumption of homoscedasticity is untenable if the expected value of the stochastic error term is assumed to be zero. Although the ordinary least-squares estimators of the regression coefficients are still unbiased, the absence of homoscedasticity results in biased estimates of the standard errors of the regression coefficients. Also the estimates of the regression coefficients would be inefficient, that is, an alternative estimation procedure could yield lower variances for the estimated coefficients. Goldberger recommends a two-step procedure. First, use ordinary least squares to obtain the calculated value of the dependent variable $\hat{y}_t$. Then use $\hat{y}_t(1 - \hat{y}_t)$ as the diagonal elements of an estimated covariance matrix and obtain generalized least-squares estimates in the second step. These estimates are not unbiased like the ordinary least-squares estimates, but they are consistent and efficient.

6. For a theoretical model in which the costs of children are a share of family income, see H. Joseph, ''Family Income Sharing and Desired Family Size,'' *Journal of Economics* 4 (1978):69-72.

6

Marriage-Pattern Influence in Procyclical and Countercyclical U.S. Fertility for Women 20-24

Lawrence R. Carter

Much of recent investigation into economic influences on fertility have shown the relationships to be procyclical. This notion has dominated even though earlier work suggests that the association was negative, at least prior to World War II.[1] Both trends are addressed by Freedman's statement that

> There is the long run secular decline in fertility associated with our transformation to an urban industrial nation. Deviations from this secular trend are strongly correlated with cyclical economic changes both in cohort analyses and in a series of time series analyses . . . there is considerable evidence for the prewar period of a negative correlation of fertility and social status as measured by occupations, education or income. . . . There was some evidence of a positive correlation with fertility at the upper end of the status scale long before the war.[2]

These studies provide sufficient ambiguity to obscure any comprehensive understanding of the relationship.

Much of the continuing debate over the economic determinants of fertility is due to inability to include the economic influence of women separately in the fertility equation or due to confounding of wives' earnings with those of husbands such that family income is seen to reflect the earnings of head of household ("Male"). A recent report by Butz and Ward has shown women's earnings to be countercyclical to fertility.[3] This work shores up strong sociological evidence that women play a significant role in decisions to bear children.

This chapter expands upon the work of Butz and Ward by analyzing the impact on fertility of income and price effects—what they define to be male income and female wage effects respectively—as influenced by the proportions of women marrying at the prime ages of marriage as well as the median age at first marriage for women. The ultimate proportion marrying is seen to be, in part, a result of demographic historicity as the populations

This research was supported in part by a Faculty Research Award from the Office of Scientific and Scholarly Research, Graduate School, University of Oregon. The author wishes to thank Rebecca Goodrich, Barbara Kosydar, Marlene McKinnon, and Alphons van de Kragt for their careful reading and preparation of this manuscript. Helpful suggestions were made by Ronald D. Lee.

71

at risk are essentially predetermined by their initial birth cohort sizes. The ultimate proportion marrying may then reflect a prevailing "marriage squeeze" or, otherwise, a surplus of males at risk to marriage. Even so, the decision to marry is thought to respond to the employment opportunities available to potential spouses. Thus economic and demographic factors are seen to influence proportions marrying. Median age at first marriage is viewed largely as a response to economic circumstances. The more favorable are the conditions, the lower the median age at first marriage. Thus demographic and economic factors are regarded as concomitants in forging marriage patterns among the young.

The analysis is distributed on birth probabilities by parity for women 20-24 years of age. This process allows the cohorts to be advanced by parity and year to note the influence of these demographic and economic determinants on birth orders for the same cohorts of women. Selecting women 20-24 years of age captures women at a major stage in the life cycle (marriage) where they are likely to be most procreative.

The analysis is separated into five parts: (1) an assessment of the Butz-Ward model by parity; (2) an investigation of the determinants of the proportions married; (3) an investigation of the determinants of the age at first marriage; (4) an incorporation of the proportions married in the Butz-Ward model; and (5) an incorporation of the age at first marriage in the Butz model. Finally, a comprehensive interpretation of this research is made with advice for future direction in this investigative effort.

Parity Distribution by the Butz-Ward Model

Butz and Ward propose an empirical economic model to provide a unified framework for reconciling the procyclical and countercyclical movements observed in time-series fertility patterns. The model encompasses two distinctions in the influences on fertility: that between male and female earnings and that between families with employed wives and those without. The model takes the following derivation:

$$\ln B = \beta_0 + \beta_1 K \cdot \ln Y_m + \beta_2 (1 - K) \cdot \ln Y_m + \beta_3 K \cdot \ln W_f$$

where

B	= the age-specific birth rate of women
Y_m	= the weighted age-specific income of men
W_f	= the estimated hourly age-specific earnings of women
K	= the age-specific proportion of women employed in the labor market
$(1 - K)$	= the age-specific proportion of women not employed in the labor market

All explanatory variables are expressed as natural logarithms weighted by some factor in K. Assuming that $\beta_1 > 0$, $\beta_2 > 0$, $\beta_3 < 0$ and collecting terms in $K \cdot \ln Y_m$, they obtain

$$\ln B = \gamma_0 + \gamma_1 K \cdot \ln Y_m + \gamma_2 \ln Y_m + \gamma_3 K \cdot \ln W_f$$

where

$$\gamma_1 = \beta_1 - \beta_2$$
$$\gamma_2 = \beta_2$$
$$\gamma_3 = \beta_3$$

The implication is that $\gamma_1 + \gamma_2 > 0$ and that the total response of the age-specific birth rates to changes in male income and female wages is, respectively, the elasticities:

$$\eta_{BY_m} = \gamma_1 K + \gamma_2 = (\beta_1 - \beta_2)K + \beta_2, \quad \text{and} \quad \eta_{BW_f} = \gamma_3 K = \beta_3 K$$

Increases in income for households have a positive income effect on fertility. However, it is the female employment ratio that constrains this effect. A low female employment ratio implies that cyclical changes in family income consist mainly of changes in men's earnings. High fertility periods reflect the extent to which high family income is expended in the costly activity of childbearing. Since wives' earnings also represent a cost of childbearing and rearing, that is, the opportunity cost of remaining home rearing children, a period of increased wages is a poor time for women to forego earnings in favor of remaining home to provide childcare. The larger the female employment ratio, the greater the likelihood that a rise in female wages will be accompanied by declining fertility rates in the population (see Butz and Ward 1977 for specifics).[4]

This model assumes that childbearing is an economically rational act subject only to market forces. It ignores the possibility of socially imposed constraints on childbearing and that those constraints are exercised through fertility expectations. Adjustments to expectations and fertility experience occur over time to regulate completed fertility to a rather narrowly defined socially acceptable range of around two to four children per household.[5] Greater understanding of procyclical and countercyclical fertility can be gained by analyzing: (1) the impact of male income and female wage effects on the consumption of children of differing birth orders and (2) the impact of prior birth orders on subsequent birth orders. Such considerations can help expose preferences for various parities within existing budget (economic) and social constraints.

This study analyzes the birth order effects of economically and socially determined fertility decisions by using birth probabilities by parity for women 20-24 years of age. This process allows the cohorts of women to be advanced by parity and year to note the influence of demographic, social, and economic determinants on birth orders for the same cohorts of women. Thus the relationship of prior birth orders to subsequent birth orders is captured. Age-parity specific birth probabilities signify the chance that women of a given parity and exact age group at the beginning of a year will have children during the year (that is, will attain the next parity before the age group advances one year). These probabilities are calculated from central birth rates and cumulative fertility rates by order. The general formula is:

$$_{n}p_{a}^{-i} = \frac{_{n}f_{a}^{i+1}}{\sum\limits_{wi}^{a+n} _{n}f_{a}^{i} - \sum\limits_{wi}^{a+n} _{n}f_{a}^{i+1}} \times 1,000$$

where

$_{n}p_{a}^{-i}$ = the age-parity specific probability

$_{n}f_{a}^{i+1}$ = i + 1th order birth rate for women of completed age a to $a + n$ years in the calendar year

$\sum\limits_{wi}^{a+n} _{n}f_{a}^{i}$ = cumulative fertility rate of order i to beginning of year for a cohort of women to exact ages a to $a + n$

$\sum\limits_{wi}^{a+n} _{n}f_{a}^{i+1}$ = cumulative fertility rate of order i + 1 to beginning of year for a cohort of exact ages a to $a + n$[6]

Retrospectively, the numerator is the number of births of order one greater than the previous order of births to women of a particular age during a specific year. The denominator is the number of women at risk to the expected age-parity specific births during that year. So the measure can be used as a reasonably satisfactory approximation of age-parity specific birth during the specified year. The analysis is confined to parities zero to four, the socially acceptable maximum, for women age 20-24. Essentially, it is a sequential disaggregation of the Butz-Ward model.

The results of this analysis are displayed in table 6-1. An operational definition of each of the variables is presented in the chapter appendix. Similar to the Butz-Ward analysis, current values of male income and female wage rates are used and caution must be exercised with respect to the

Table 6-1
Regressions of Age-Specific Birth Rate and Parities for Women Age 20-24, 1948-1974

Independent Variables	Age Specific lnB	Parities			
		lnB_1	lnB_2	lnB_3	lnB_4
$K \cdot \ln Y_m$	−.456	−.308	−.448	−.519	−.385
	(−3.20)	(−1.90)	(−3.49)	(−4.42)	(−3.22)
$K \cdot \ln W_f$	−1.577	−1.219	−1.398	−1.390	−1.107
	(−2.17)	(−1.48)	(−2.15)	(−2.33)	(−1.83)
$\ln Y_m$	.846	.496	.986	.704	.122
	(4.12)	(2.13)	(5.36)	(4.17)	(.713)
Intercept	.298	2.241	−.639	1.726	6.072
	(.21)	(1.38)	(−.498)	(1.47)	(5.08)
$\bar{R}^2$	.91	.83	.90	.95	.95
D.W. statistic	.54	.44	.57	.66	.70

Note: The reported $\bar{R}^2$s are based on instruments. Numbers in parentheses are (asymptotic) t statistics. Degrees of freedom are (3, 23).

specification of the model. The variables $K \cdot \ln Y_m$ and $K \cdot \ln W_f$ are treated as endogenous to allow comparability with the Butz-Ward results. The model performs well as evidenced in the elasticities shown in table 6-2. The age-specific fertility outcome is consistent with the Butz-Ward results. Positive income effects are shown for all parities except $\ln B_4$, and negative female wage effects exist for all parities. The strongest of both positive and negative effects are for parity $\ln B_2$ indicating perhaps that the second child is pivotal for expectations about completed family size. The declining impact of both effects after parity $\ln B_2$ may indicate the lessening influence of economic factors for these births, though only the income effects for $\ln B_4$ post a substantial change in the elasticity. Though the $\bar{R}^2$s, are high, the D.W.s indicate serious autocorrelation of disturbances. So the estimator values and the t ratios must be regarded with caution.

Table 6-2
Population-Elasticity Estimates

Elasticity of Fertility Rate with Respect to	Age Specific lnB	Parities			
		lnB_1	lnB_2	lnB_3	lnB_4
Male income effects	.636	.354	.779	.465	−.055
Female wage effects	−.727	−.562	−.644	−.641	−.510

Proportions Married

Marriage is in part membership in a union in which coitus and reproduction are socially sanctioned. At the societal level then the reproductive potential and actual fertility experience of a country is partially determined "by the age distribution of its female population and sociocultural forces that shape variations in age at marriage and the proportions marrying."[7] Consequently, most childbearing occurs within marriage, and so age-specific proportions married is a good measure of the percent of the population in a particular age group subject to risk of fertility. As such, it is an important intermediate variable in the Davis-Blake analytical scheme detailing the variables intervening culture and fertility.[8] Since proportions married is essential to understanding fertility levels, it seems likewise important to understand the determinants of the proportions marrying.

The importance of this variable is apparent when it is considered in light of relatively recent countercyclical fertility decline. According to Glick and Norton the annual first-marriage rate has been in an almost continuous decline for two decades.[9] This decline is reflected in the proportions of women remaining single at ages 20-24; a rise by one half since 1960, from 28 percent to 43 percent.

Several reasons have been advanced for the decline. A major factor was the Vietnam war. Military service caused many young men to postpone marriage, while others delayed marriage by remaining in school to avoid induction into the armed forces. At the same time many young single women remained in higher education or became experienced members of the labor force. These experiences created greater independence among them while offering alternatives to the traditional expectations for early marriage, homemaking, and childrearing.

Another source of postponement was a developing "marriage squeeze" where the number of women reaching the usual age of first marriage for women (18-24) was in excess of eligible men (20-26) by 5 to 10 percent. Glick attributes this "marriage squeeze" to the baby boom and the fact that first-time grooms are typically two to three years older than their brides. With staggered-age pairings, as the baby boom began to peak (1957), each cohort of girls born each year exceeded the numbers of its potential spouses born in cohorts two to three years earlier.

Finally, because of the large sizes of the baby-boom cohorts, there is unbearable pressure on the labor market that is unable to absorb them. The stiff competition for jobs has created a pessimism among many youth about being able to provide for a family. Consequently, there is greater postponement of entry into first marriages.[10] All these factors and more perhaps have contributed to the decline in proportions marrying. Though we consider all marriages for the population age 20-24 (that is, first marriages and remarriages), it should be understood that while the remarriage rate is higher than the first-marriage rate, the bulk of the proportions married age 20-24 constitutes first marriages.

The weight of economic factors is apparent in these arguments. Economists have attempted to deduce such relationships from a nascent economic theory of marriage. The theory has been used to analyze various economic aspects of marriage and marital instability, that is, marriage, divorce, and remarriage.[11] The theory assumes that individuals have underlying sets of preferences; that marriage is almost always a voluntary act among partners (or contrived by their parents); and that spouses expect to obtain a utility level in marriage greater than would be experienced if each remained single. In addition, a marriage market is presumed to exist in which men and women compete to find best mates, subject to the restrictions imposed by market conditions.[12]

The theory also assumes that, though certain economies of scale are secured in household formation, the reasons for marriage extend beyond these gains. Marriage stems from the socially endorsed "rights" to raise own children and to intimacy (loving and caring) intended in such a bonding. Given these endorsements, marriage is secured to the extent that economies of scale are produced. Becker uses his formulation of the theory to analyse the determinants of the gain from marriage, the sorting of men and women into marital pairings by market and nonmarket characteristics, and the division of total output of a household between husband and wife.

Given the selectivity of factors just reviewed as contributing to the decline in proportions marrying, this analysis concentrates on Becker's treatment of assortive mating between men and women. Specifically, the impact of negative assortive mating in earnings is investigated. Becker argues that "positive assortive mating—a positive correlation between the values of the traits of husbands and wives is generally optimal. . . ."[13] Positive assortive mating is usually reflected in such characteristics as intelligence, education, attractiveness, skin color, ethnic origin, height, and so on.[14] Negative assortive mating in earnings (that is, a negative relationship between the earnings of husbands and wives) is the exception that is, too, optimal. The reason for this exception is that both complementarity and substitution can be optimal for household production. Whereas qualitative equality in characteristics is seen as reinforcing and thus complementary, qualitative inequality in a trait such as earnings between spouses can be offsetting as substitution.

Optimal negative assortive mating in earnings reinforces division of labor in the household since it allows for the substitution of nonmarket time for market time in household production activity. In marriage, men typically spend more time in the market sector where they specialize in acquiring skills that raise market productivity compared to nonmarket productivity.

Women's time investments generally have been geared more to nonmarket activities such as childrearing, household management, and other domestic activities. Consequently, optimal negative sorting would imply that men with high earnings potential would marry women with relatively low earnings potential but with superior nonmarket characteristics and vice versa.[15] The prevailing mode has been to concentrate market activity among husbands and nonmarket activity among wives. This mutual reinforcement of husband's market activity and wife's nonmarket activity is, for Becker, economically beneficial. "For," he states, "nonmarket productivity and money income tend to combine multiplicatively, so that higher values of a trait have larger absolute effects when combined with higher income."[16]

Accordingly, since many factors appear to contribute to or impede the propensity to marry young (at 20-24 years of age), a number of relationships thought to affect negative assortative mating in earnings are tested to seek a best approximation to the causal framework. Only the first equation conforms to the Butz-Ward components. The other equations are designed to capture some of the marriage-related factors just discussed. All analysis of equations 2 through 5 is by OLS. The equations are:

1. $\ln M_f = F(K \cdot \ln Y_m, K \cdot \ln W_f, \ln Y_m)$

2. $\ln M_f = F(\ln LPR_{m_1}, \ln LPR_{m_2}, \ln LPR_f, \ln SR)$

3. $\ln M_f = F(\ln LPR_{m_1}, \ln LPR_{m_2}, \ln LPR_f, \ln CPI)$

4. $\ln M_f = F(\ln LPR_{m_1}, \ln LPR_{m_2}, \ln UNEMP_f, \ln SR)$

5. $\ln M_f = F(\ln LPR_{m_1}, \ln LPR_{m_2}, \ln LPR_f, \ln SR, \ln CPI)$

where

$\ln M_f$ = proportions of women married age 20-24

$\ln LPR_{m_1}$ = labor-force participation rate, males, age 20-24

$\ln LPR_{m_2}$ = labor-force participation rate, males, age 25-34

$\ln LPR_f$ = labor-force participation rate, females, age 20-24

$\ln UNEMP_f$ = unemployment rate, women, age 20-24

$\ln SR$ = single sex ratio, weighted for men ages 20-24, 25-29, 30-34

$\ln CPI$ = consumer price index

Drawing on Glick's comments and Becker's analysis, the proportions female married should respond to the explanatory variables in the following manner in sign:

$$K \cdot \ln Y_m \ (-) \qquad \ln LPR_{m_1} \ (+) \qquad \ln UNEMP_f \ (+)$$

$$K \cdot \ln W_f \ (-) \qquad \ln LPR_{m_2} \ (+) \qquad \ln SR \qquad (+)$$

$$\ln Y_m \ (+) \qquad \ln LPR_f \ (-) \qquad \ln CPI \qquad (-)$$

These relationships posit that any factors that draw women into the labor force ($K \cdot \ln Y_m$, $K \cdot \ln W_f$, and $\ln LPR_f$) will induce resistance to marriage since to do so would not be optimal for household productivity. Alternatively, factors that imply male market productivity ($\ln LPR_{m_1}$ and $\ln LPR_{m_2}$) or female market nonproductivity ($\ln UNEMP_f$) should promote marriage. The single sex ratio is a measure of the relative supply of men and women in the appropriate age group at risk to marriage. Since women age 20-24 tend to marry older men in the proportions (.65, .23, .05) to ages (20-24, 25-29, 30-34), respectively, the numerator of $\ln SR$ is so constructed. For the same reasons, $\ln LPR_{m_2}$ is included. Women should respond positively to $\ln SR$. Finally, $\ln CPI$ is included to reflect changes in the real purchasing power of household earnings. Increases in $\ln CPI$ should prompt hesitance among marriageable women.

The results are shown in table 6-3. It is apparent that the proportion female married ($\ln M_f$) responds differently to the explanatory variables ($K \cdot \ln Y_m$, $K \cdot \ln W_f$, $\ln Y_m$) in equation 1 than do births in table 6-1. Female wage effects are not significant. The elasticity for male income effects is .054, considerably less than obtained for any birth variable in table 6-1. The remaining equations perform considerably better. Among them, the consistently strong indicators are the labor-force participation rates. Only in equation 4 is the sign for $\ln LPR_{m_1}$ as anticipated. No explanation for the reversed signs is apparent.

Female unemployment has minimal and unreliable negative impact on female marriage. The sex ratio performs as anticipated, though it is a weak indicator and not significant in equation 2. The consumer price index performs as anticipated, though it too is a rather weak indicator for proportions female married. The consumer price index is an inconsistent and reliable indicator of relative costs of commodities that should argue negatively for marriage.

What this analysis shows is that births and proportions female married have different response patterns to male income effects and female wage effects, and so they do not provide a formula for the two related phenomena. What these results suggest is that labor-force participation rate and, to a lesser degree, the sex ratio of single men and women may provide greater richness in understanding the marriage process. Nevertheless, all the equations experience serious autocorrelated error and should be regarded with caution.

Table 6-3
Regressions of Proportions Married for Women Age 20-24, 1950-1974

| Independent Variables | lnMf | | | | |
	(1)	(2)	(3)	(4)	(5)
$K \cdot \ln Y_m$	−.153 (−9.00)				
$K \cdot \ln W_f$	.001 (.01)				
$\ln Y_m$	.125 (3.46)				
$\ln LPR_{m_1}$		−.502 (−2.39)	−.522 (−3.09)	.592 (2.18)	−.503 (−2.81)
$\ln LPR_{m_2}$		2.23 (3.18)	1.822 (3.83)	5.938 (6.80)	1.503 (2.50)
$\ln LPR_f$		−.504 (−7.44)	−.562 (−7.66)		−.394 (−4.82)
$\ln UNEMP_f$				−.031 (−1.25)	
$\ln SR$		.041 (1.63)		.196 (3.31)	.067 (3.01)
$\ln CPI$			.024 (.60)		−.08 (−1.52)
Intercept	3.738 (13.74)	−1.800 (−.46)	.288 (.119)	−25.60 (−6.64)	1.453 (.43)
$\bar{R}^2$	.96	.98	.98	.94	.99
D.W. statistic	1.00	1.21	1.30	1.20	1.35

Note: The reported $\bar{R}^2$s for equation 1 are based on instruments. The remaining $\bar{R}^2$s are calculated for OLS. The degrees of freedom are, respectively, (3, 20), (4, 19), (4, 19), (4, 19), and (5, 18).

Age at First Marriage

A current and common idea expressed about childbearing is that a decline in the age at first marriage is related to a decline in the age at first childbearing which promotes higher cohort period fertility.[17] Most women marry between the ages of 20-24. Since most childbearing occurs within these ages, the earlier the age at first marriage to women in this age group, the longer their exposure to risk of childbearing during their most procreative years. If these relationships are true, then an understanding of the determinants of the age at first marriage would provide clearer understanding of consequent fertility.

According to Dixon, the age at marriage for women is affected by three factors: (1) the availability of marriage partners, which is influenced by age and sex ratios in the marriage market; (2) the feasibility of marriage, which is influenced in large part by financial opportunities and constraints; and (3) the desirability of marriage in terms of how each partner sees the relative advantages and disadvantages of marriage compared with the available alternatives.[18] In this light, the arguments presented earlier to explain increases and declines in the proportions marrying are seen likewise to influence the age at first marriage. Favorable conditions should reduce the age at first marriage, while unfavorable conditions should prompt waiting.

Davis suggests that additional factors promoting earlier marriages are social supports in the form of social services and subsidies and prolonged parental support to couples long after they are married.[19] These supports make marriage a less fateful commitment, and the lowered risk of failure should induce couples to marry at an earlier age. Accordingly, since males have had primarily economic responsibility for marriages, he finds (by 1972) that groom's median age at first marriage has declined more than the brides. However, he also believes the increasing social and economic independence for women induces them to delay marriage. Since the concern here is for the fertility-related behavior of women, age at first marriage of women is the focus in this section.

Median age at first marriage is regressed on the same factors as in the previous section. The relationships are:

1. $\ln AFM_f = F(K \cdot \ln Y_m, K \cdot \ln W_f, \ln Y_m)$
2. $\ln M_f = (\ln LPR_{m_1}, \ln LPR_{m_2}, \ln LPR_f, \ln SR)$
3. $\ln M_f = (\ln LPR_{m_1}, \ln LPR_{m_2}, \ln LPR_f, \ln CPI)$
4. $\ln M_f = (\ln LPR_{m_1}, \ln LPR_{m_2}, \ln UNEMP_f, \ln SR)$
5. $\ln M_f = (\ln LPR_{m_1}, \ln LPR_{m_2}, \ln LPR_f, \ln SR, \ln CPI)$

Here $\ln AFM_f$ is the median age at first marriage for women. The expected signs are:

$K \cdot \ln Y_m$ (+)	$\ln LPR_{m_1}$ (−)	$\ln UNEMP_f$ (−)
$K \cdot \ln W_f$ (+)	$\ln LPR_{m_2}$ (−)	$\ln SR$ (−)
$\ln Y_m$ (−)	$\ln LPR_f$ (+)	$\ln CPI$ (+)

Expected signs are opposite those anticipated in the relationships for proportions married.

Note in table 6-4 that the explanatory variables perform less well than in table 6-3. In equation 1, male income effects were thought to be positive and they are not (elasticity − .012) and are almost nonexistent. Female wage effects are minimal but positive as anticipated (elasticity .016). The equation does not explain well. Among the remaining equations, the only consistent and significant variable is $\ln LPR_f$. The male labor-force participation

Table 6-4

Regressions of Age at First Marriage for Women Age 20-24, 1950-1974

Independent Variables	$lnAFMf$				
	(1)	(2)	(3)	(4)	(5)
$K \cdot lnY_m$	.029 (4.59)				
$K \cdot lnW_f$	.039 (.97)				
lnY_m	−.025 (−2.45)				
$lnLPR_{m_1}$		−.070 (−.81)	−.117 (−2.34)	−.304 (−3.97)	−.112 (−1.16)
$lnLPR_{m_2}$		−.233 (−.78)	−.110 (−.629)	−1.093 (−4.53)	−.233 (−.721)
$lnLPR_f$		.102 (3.65)	.111 (3.63)		.093 (2.12)
$lnUNEMP_f$				.003 (.45)	
$lnSR$				−.031 (−1.83)	−.009 (−.77)
$lnCPI$			−.007 (−.46)		−.002 (−.06)
Intercept	3.111 (39.86)	4.000 (2.38)	3.648 (4.78)	9.381 (8.65)	4.230 (2.36)
$\bar{R}^2$	.89	.95	.93	.91	.93
D.W. statistic	1.25	1.87	1.91	1.47	1.79

Note: The reported $\bar{R}^2$s for equation 1 are based on instruments. The remaining $\bar{R}^2$s are calculated for OLS. The degrees of freedom are, respectively, (3, 20), (4, 19), (4, 19), (4, 19), and (5, 18).

rates have the anticipated sign but are erratic in their significances. The remaining variables are meaningless indicators. The R^2s are uniformly high. Equations 2, 3, and 5 evidence no serious autocorrelated error. Again these equations indicate that among them only labor-force participation rates offer any semblance of understanding of age at first marriage.

Proportions Married in the Butz-Ward Equations

Since most childbearing occurs within marriage, these unions are, as stated earlier, important intermediate variables in understanding the relationship of culture to fertility. An earlier section showed only a tenuous identification of some factors underlying marriage propositions for women age 20-24. Among them, only labor-force participation rates are strong indicators, while the sex ratio offers a limited contribution. The low D.W.s suggest autocorrelated error and thus questionable interpretability of their contributions.

Here, proportions married are related to birth parities in the presence of male income effect and female wage effects. These effects were shown to be good indicators of fertility experience. The question now is whether marriage adds significantly to the explanatory power of the equations. The equation takes the general form:

$$\ln B_i = \gamma_{0_i} + \eta_i K \cdot \ln Y_m + \gamma_{2_i} \ln Y_m + \gamma_{3_i} K \cdot \ln W_f + \gamma_{4_i} \ln M_f \quad i = (1, ..., 4)$$

(The equation for $\ln B$ is used as a reference.)

The results are shown in table 6-5. The introduction of $\ln M_f$ into these equations serves to reduce substantially the influence of the remaining explanatory variables. The marriage variable is strong and significant in each instance. However, though the R^2s are consistently high, the D.W.s are low, indicating serious autocorrelated error. The estimators are therefore unstable and the t ratios unreliable measures of significance.

Why the seemingly strong relationship of marriage to fertility? It has been posited in this analysis that year-to-year fluctuations in birth parities, though shown by Butz and Ward to be due to male income effects and female wage effects, are, in addition, responses to changes in frequency of marriage. Lee explains that marital fertility and marriage frequency are highly correlated but respond to similar disturbances.[20] This analysis has

Table 6-5
Regressions of Age-Specific Births and Parities for Women Age 20-24, 1951-1974, Impact of Proportions Married

Independent Variables	Age Specific $\ln B$	Parities			
		$\ln B_1$	$\ln B_2$	$\ln B_3$	$\ln B_4$
$\ln M_f$	4.507	3.712	3.056	3.276	2.353
	(3.45)	(6.81)	(6.97)	(5.91)	(4.24)
$K \cdot \ln Y_m$	.107	.186	.024	−.041	−.065
	(.52)	(1.187)	(.19)	(−.26)	(−.41)
$K \cdot \ln W_f$	−.537	−.777	−1.051	−1.180	−.828
	(−.89)	(−1.02)	(−2.02)	(−1.79)	(−1.26)
$\ln Y_m$	−.171	−.070	.264	.189	−.23
	(−.693)	(−.26)	(1.22)	(.69)	(−.85)
Intercept	−12.500	−10.574	−9.313	−9.592	−2.096
	(−2.29)	(−3.60)	(−3.94)	(−3.21)	(−.70)
$\bar{R}^2$	.94	.92	.95	.95	.95
D.W. statistic	1.01	.80	1.33	1.08	.97

Note: The reported $\bar{R}^2$s are based on instruments. Numbers in parentheses are (asymptotic) t statistics. Degrees of freedom are (4, 19).

not shown the common causes to be male income effects, nor female wage effects. So the underlying explanation remains to be found.

Age at First Marriage in the Butz-Ward Equations

The final analysis draws the median age at first marriage for women into the Butz-Ward equation. We follow on the assertions of Coale and others that age at first marriage should be negatively related to fertility.[21] Since most childbearing occurs within marriage and since most first marriages are contracted between the ages 20-24 for women, fluctuations in the marriage age in this interval should manifest fluctuations in period fertility for these cohorts. From the earlier analysis of the determinants of age at first marriage, male income effects and female wage effects are assumed to be additive with age at marriage in explaining fertility by parity. The general form of the equation is:

$$\ln B_i = \gamma_{0_i} + \gamma_{1_i} K \cdot \ln Y_m + \gamma_{2_i} K \cdot \ln W_f + \gamma_{3_i} \ln Y_m + \gamma_{4_i} \ln AFM_f, i = (1, ..., 4)$$

(Again the equation for $\ln B$ is used for reference.)

The findings are displayed in table 6-6. The disturbing pattern of table 6-5 is duplicated. The age-at-first marriage variable shows high magnitude, strong significance, and the proper sign. The influence of male income effects and female wage effects are critically suppressed. None of these variables is significant, and the shifting signs indicate the instability of the estimators. The R^2s are high and rather uniform. However, the low D.W.s argue for significant autocorrelated error and questionable interpretability of the model.

All equations incorporating the endogenous explanatory variables $K \cdot \ln Y$ and $K \cdot \ln W$ are two-stage, least-squares estimates. For these equations, $\ln Y_m$, $\ln Y^f_{m_{t-1}}$, $\ln W_f$, and $\ln W_{f_{t-1}}$ were employed as instruments in prior estimates of the endogenous explanatory variables. This procedure is in keeping with the formulation used by Butz and Ward. Equations employing lagged explanatory variables are attached (tables 6-7 and 6-8). They perform less well than regressors contemporaneous with the dependent variables. The remaining equations are ordinary least-squares estimates since two-stage formulations have not been satisfactorily modeled by the author. They are exploratory efforts.

Summary and Conclusions

This study attempted to analyze the influence of marriage patterns in the United States on procyclical and countercyclical fertility for women age

Table 6-6
Regressions of Age-Specific Births and Parities for Women Age 20-24, 1951-1974, Impact of Age at First Marriage

Independent Variables	Age Specific lnB	Parities			
		lnB_1	lnB_2	lnB_3	lnB_4
$lnAFM_f$	−8.114	−15.127	−9.901	−10.39	−8.469
	(−1.69)	(−3.80)	(−3.30)	(−3.08)	(−2.79)
$K \cdot lnY_m$	−.294	.052	−.148	−.230	−.177
	(−1.39)	(.238)	(−.90)	(−1.25)	(−1.06)
$K \cdot lnW_f$	−.777	−.359	−.786	−.903	−.598
	(−1.18)	(−.39)	(−1.13)	(−1.16)	(−.85)
lnY_m	.549	.223	.500	.441	−.051
	(2.02)	(.59)	(1.75)	(1.38)	(−.18)
Intercept	26.518	48.678	32.05	34.109	32.211
	(1.82)	(4.11)	(3.58)	(3.39)	(3.56)
$\bar{R}^2$	.92	.84	.92	.94	.94
D.W. statistics	1.25	1.23	1.33	1.22	1.16

Note: The reported $\bar{R}^2$s are based on instruments. Numbers in parentheses are (asymptotic) t statistics. Degrees of freedom are (4, 19).

20-24. Its purpose was to expand on the impact of male income effects and female wage effects on fertility as interpreted by Butz and Ward in their paper, "The Emergence of Countercyclical U.S. Fertility." The analysis was done in five stages: (1) an assessment of the Butz-Ward model by pari-

Table 6-7
Regressions of Age-Specific Birth Rate and Parities for Women Age 20-24, 1948-1974, Using Lagged Explanatory Variables

Independent Variables	Total lnB	Parities			
		lnB_1	lnB_2	lnB_3	lnB_4
$K \cdot lnY_{m_{t-1}}$	1.084	−.13	1.002	−.170	.645
	(.244)	(−.16)	(6.02)	(−2.00)	(3.19)
$K \cdot lnW_{f_{t-1}}$	−1.110	−.133	.209	−.578	−.415
	(−1.21)	(−.16)	(.36)	(−.95)	(−.59)
$lnY_{m_{t-1}}$	−.379	−.06	.134	−.170	−.527
	(−1.84)	(−.60)	(1.66)	(−2.00)	(−5.38)
Intercept	6.222	1.98	−.853	1.325	6.432
	(2.60)	(1.77)	(−1.07)	(1.57)	(6.63)
$\bar{R}^2$	.90	.95	.98	.99	.98
D.W. statistic	.59	.50	.59	.79	.89

Note: The reported $\bar{R}^2$s are based on instruments. Numbers in parentheses are (asymptotic) t statistics. Degrees of freedom are (3, 23).

Table 6-8

Regressions of Age-Specific Births and Parities for Women Age 20-24, 1948-1974, Impact of Proportions Married, Lagged Explanatory Variables

Independent Variables	Age Specific lnB	Parities			
		lnB_1	lnB_2	lnB_3	lnB_4
lnM_f	2.964	4.010	3.195	3.265	2.253
	(2.05)	(6.44)	(6.08)	(4.48)	(3.04)
$K \cdot lnY_m$	−.172	.147	−.069	−.074	−.030
	(−.48)	(.88)	(−.49)	(−.38)	(−.15)
$K \cdot lnW_f$	−.465	−.167	−.484	−.962	−.894
	(−.353)	(−.24)	(−.82)	(−1.18)	(−1.08)
lnY_m	.164	−.296	−.137	−.016	−.473
	(.44)	(−1.13)	(.620)	(−.52)	(−1.52)
Intercept	−7.741	−9.911	−8.590	−7.786	.138
	(−1.54)	(−3.08)	(−3.16)	(−2.06)	(.036)
$\bar{R}^2$	.92	.92	.94	.93	.93
D.W. statistic	1.08	1.08	1.08	1.07	1.04

Note: The reported $\bar{R}^2$s are based on instruments. Numbers in parentheses are (asymptotic) t statistics. Degrees of freedom are (4, 22).

ty; (2) an investigation of the determinants of the proportions married; (3) an investigation of the determinants of the age at first marriage; (4) an incorporation of proportions married in the Butz-Ward model; and (5) an incorporation of the age at first marriage in the Butz-Ward model.

Of the five stages, the first was the most successful as it was shown that the model was consistent over parities one through four. The other stages were somewhat disappointing as the determinants of the marriage factors either could not be adequately identified or the introduction of the marriage factors seriously distorted the basic equation. Labor-force participation rates and, more limitedly, the sex ratio seem to contribute to an explanation of proportions married. Only labor-force participation rates were indicative for age at first marriage. Among these significant variables the female-categorized variable was opposite the male-categorized variables, indicating some sex differentiation in orientation to marriage and to fertility decision making. Introducing the marriage factors into the basic Butz-Ward model reduced the male income effects and the female wage effects substantially. Proportions married did appear to be procyclical, while age at marriage was countercyclical, suggesting that greater independence for women is likely to augur for reduced marital fertility.

Much of the disappointment in the findings can be attributed to methodological problems. Though the R^2s were high, serious autocorrelated error was rampant in all of the equations except in stage 3 where the determinants of age at first marriage were investigated. High autocorrelation renders the estimators unstable and the *t* ratios unreliable. So caution must be exercised in interpreting most of the results. However, autocorrelated error was manifest in the original Butz-Ward study from which the basic model here was desired. In addition, many of these equations were analyzed using OLS as exploratory efforts because formulations allowing for reciprocal causality had not been satisfactorily modeled. Thus these analyses are merely a first step in explicating sex-differentiated determinants of marital fertility. This study is presently being replicated by the author with conditions of stationarity imposed to ascertain the nature of the relationships with autocorrelated disturbances removed. Reciprocal causality is being addressed in the refined models. Greater confidence in the results should eventuate.

What the study does suggest is that fluctuations in proportions married and age at first marriage are only indirectly related to fluctuations in fertility. For though they all appear highly correlated, their determinants appear to be different. The high autocorrelation in most of the equations indicate that both regressors and dependent variables are responding to some exogenous phenomenon that is not captured in the equations. If so, then the quest should be to find a unified formula that encapsulates and explicates that phenomenon in a way that more adequately relates marriage patterns to procyclical and countercyclical fertility.

Notes

1. Examples of procyclical work are Gary S. Becker, "An Economic Analysis of Fertility," in *Demographic and Economic Change in Developed Countries*, ed. Universities—National Bureau Committee for Economic Research (Princeton, N.J.: Princeton University Press, 1960, pp. 209-231; Richard A. Easterlin, "Relative Economic Status and the American Fertility Swing," in *Family Economic Behavior*, ed. Eleanor B. Sheldon (Philadelphia: Lippincott, 1973); Richard A. Easterlin, *The Economics and Sociology of Fertility: A Synthesis* (rev. ed.) (Philadelphia: University of Pennsylvania Press, 1973). Some of the earlier countercyclical works are: Dudley Kirk and Dorothy L. Nortman, "Business and Babies: The Influence of the Business Cycle on Birth Rates," *Proceedings of the Social Statistics Section, American Statistical Association*, 1958, 151-160; Virginia L. Gailbraith and Dorothy S. Thomas, "Birth Rates and Inter-war Business Cycles," *Journal of the American Statistical Association* 36 (1941):465-476; William F. Ogburn and Dorothy S. Thomas, "The Influence of the Business Cycle on Certain Social Conditions," *Quarterly Publications of the American Statistical Association* 18 (1922):324-340; Alan Sweezy, "The Economic Explanation of Fertility Changes in the United States," *Population Studies* 25 (1970):255-267.

2. Ronald Freedman, "American Studies of Family Planning and Fertility: A Review of Major Trends and Issues," *Research in Family Planning*, ed. C.V. Kiser (Princeton, N.J.: Princeton University Press, 1962), p. 212.

3. William P. Butz and Michael P. Ward, *The Emergence of Counter-cyclical U.S. Fertility* (The Rand Corporation, R-1605-NIH, 1977).

4. Ibid.

5. Judith Blake, "Are Babies Consumer Durables," *Population Studies* 22 (1962):5-26; Judith Blake, "Ideal Family Size among White Americans: A Quarter of A Century's Evidence," *Demography* 3 (1966):154-173; Norman B. Ryder and Charles F. Westoff, *Reproduction in the United States: 1965* (Princeton: Princeton University Press, 1971); Pascal K. Whelpton, Arthur A. Campbell, and John E. Patterson, *Fertility and Family Planning in the United States* (Princeton: Princeton University Press, 1966); Janet Griffith, "Social Pressure on Family Size Intentions," *Family Planning Perspectives* 5 (1973):237-242; James T. Fawcett, et al., *The Value of Children in Asia and the United States: Comparative Perspectives* (Honolulu: The East-West Center, 1974).

6. Henry Shryock and Jacob S. Siegel, *The Methods and Materials of Demography* (condensed edition by Edward Stockwell) (New York: Academic Press, 1976).

7. Calvin Goldscheider, *Population, Modernization, and Social Structure* (Boston: Little, Brown, 1971), p. 227.

8. Kingsley Davis and Judith Blake, "Social Structure and Flexibility: An Analytical Framework," *Economic Development and Cultural Change* 4 (1956):212.

9. Paul C. Glick and Arthur J. Norton, "Marrying, Divorcing and Living Together in the U.S. Today," *Population Bulletin*, 32, no. 5 (Washington, D.C.: Population Reference Bureau, 1977).

10. Ibid., pp. 5-6.

11. Gary S. Becker, "A Theory of Marriage," in *Economics of the Family: Marriage, Children, and Human Capital*, ed. T.W. Schultz (Chicago: The University of Chicago Press for the National Bureau of Economic Research, 1974); Gary S. Becker, Elizabeth M. Landes, and Robert T. Michael, "An Economic Analysis of Marital Instability," *Journal of Political Economy* 85 (1977):1141-1187.

12. Becker, "A Theory of Marriage," p. 300.

13. Ibid., p. 300.

14. Ibid., p. 300.

15. Becker, Landes, and Michael, "An Economic Analysis of Marital Instability," p. 1146.

16. Ibid.

17. Ansley J. Coale, "Alternative Paths to a Stationary Population," in U.S. Commission on Population Growth and the American Future,

Demographic and Social Aspects of Population Growth, ed. Charles F. Westoff and Robert Parke, Jr., vol. 1 of *Commission Research Reports* (Washington, D.C.: Government Printing Office, 1972), 589-266.

18. Alice Henry and Phyllis T. Protrow, "Age at Marriage and Fertility," *Population Reports* M(4) (1979):105-160.

19. Kingsley Davis, "The American Family in Relation to Demographic Change," in U.S. Commission of Population Growth and the American Future, *Demographic and Social Aspects of Population Growth*, eds. Charles F. Westoff and Robert Parke, Jr., vol. 1 of *Commission Research Reports* (Washington, D.C.: Government Printing Office, 1972), 235-266.

20. Ronald D. Lee, "Natural Fertility, Population Cycles and the Spectral Analysis of Births and Marriages," *Journal of the American Statistical Association* 70 (1975):295-304.

21. Coale, "Alternative Paths to a Stationary Population."

Appendix 6A
Definitions of Basic
Variables in Tables 6-1
through 6-8

B Age-specific fertility rate for women age 20-24. (Source: William P. Butz and Michael P. Ward, *The Emergence of Countercyclical U.S. Fertility*, The Rand Corporation, R-1605-NIH, 1977).

$\ln B_i$ Birth probabilities for all women age 20-24 in years 1948-1974 by age and parity for groups of cohorts from 1924-1928 to 1950-1954. (Source: *Fertility Tables for Birth Cohorts by Color, United States, 1917-73*, Table 9A augmented for 1974 with estimates by Robert Heuser, NCHS.)

Y_m For women 20-24, this is .57 times median income of males age 20-24 plus .43 times median income of males age 25-34. The weights reflect the probability that a child born to a woman age 20-24 has a father age 25-34 at the time of the child's birth. (Source: Butz and Ward, *The Emergence of Countercyclical U.S. Fertility*.)

W_f Estimated hourly earnings of women age 20-24. This measure is the median annual income of these women divided by the estimated number of hours worked in the year. (Source: Butz and Ward, *The Emergence of Countercyclical U.S. Fertility*.)

K Number of women age 20-24 employed in the labor market at any time during the year divided by the number of women of those ages: the female employment ratio. (Source: Butz and Ward, *The Emergence of Countercyclical U.S. Fertility*.)

M_f Proportions married of women age 20-24. This measure is a three-year moving average of the percent married of women age 20-24 (personal correspondence, Campbell Gibson, U.S. Bureau of the Census). (Source: *Current Population Reports, Series P-20, Marital Status and Household Characteristics*, Table 1, various issues).

AFM_f Median age at first marriage for women age 20-24. (Source: *Current Population Reports, Series P-20, Marital Status and Living Arrangements*, Table A, various issues.)

LPR_{m_i} Labor-force participation rates for men age 20-24 ($i = 1$) and 25-34 ($i = 2$). (Source: *Handbook of Labor Statistics 1970*, Washington, D.C.: Government Printing Office, 1971; *Handbook of Labor Statistics 1977*, Washington, D.C.: Government Printing Office, 1978, Table 54.)

LPR$_f$ Labor-force participation rates for women age 20-24. (Source: *Handbook of Labor Statistics*, 1970 and 1977, Table 54.)

UNEMP$_f$ Unemployment rates for women 20-24. (Source: *Handbook of Labor Statistics*, 1970 and 1977, Table 69.)

SR   Sex ratio for single men age 20-34 to single women age 20-24. The numerator is a weighted measure of .65 times number of single men age 20-24 plus .23 times number of single men age 25-29 plus .05 times number of single men age 30-34. This measure represents the total number of single men weighted in the proportions in which they are married by women age 20-24. The denominator is the number of single women age 20-24. (Source: *Current Population Reports, Series P-20, Marital Status and Household Characteristics*, Table 1, various issues, and *Vital Statistics of the U.S., Marriage and Divorce*, vol. 2, tables 1-22, various issues.)

CPI   Consumer Price Index. (Source: *Economic Report of the President*, Washington, D.C.: Government Printing Office, 1979.)

Part III
Public-Policy Concerns

7

The Negative Income-Tax Experiments: Some Reflections on Their Implications for a Theory of the Family

John Bishop

Introduction

For many years it has been thought that one of the primary ways in which public policy might be designed to strengthen families was to expand eligibility for welfare benefits to include two-parent families. When, however, this policy was implemented in the Negative Income Tax (NIT) experiments, we discovered that exactly the opposite happened. Two-parent families eligible for NIT cash assistance experienced marital dissolution rates that over a three-year period were 30 to 40 percent higher than the control group that was eligible for the current set of income-maintenance programs—food stamps, AFDC, and AFDC-UP. This chapter explores the implications of these startling findings for (1) the design of income-maintenance programs and economic policy generally and for (2) theories of the family and marital instability. The first two sections of the paper review the empirical literature on the impact of income-maintenance programs on marital instability. The third section compares the pattern of NIT experimental responses to the prediction of income-maintenance impacts provided by the highly simplified theoretical models used in much of the previous research. The discovery of important discrepancies leads to a rejection of that very simple model and a search for elaborations and modifications of theory that fit the data better. Six alternative modifications of theory are proposed, and the evidence for and against each one is outlined.

Under an assumption that society would like to minimize the marital destabilizing effects of its social and economic policies, the fourth section proceeds to develop the policy implications of the NIT findings. The fifth section returns to the discussion of the implications of the NIT findings for theories of marriage and divorce and sketches the outline of a possible complete reconstruction of the theory.

Nonexperimental Studies of the Relation between
Welfare and Marital Instability

Current welfare programs make most low-income, two-parent families ineligible for the Medicaid and AFDC support that similarly situated one-parent families receive. Sometimes the earnings of a father are less than the value of the food stamps, AFDC, and Medicaid his family would become eligible for if he were to desert them.

While it may seem only logical that these perverse incentives should increase marital instability, the empirical evidence for the proposition is by no means secure. Honig found a positive relationship between the level of the AFDC payment and rates of female headship for blacks and whites in both 1960 and 1970.[1] The effect is not statistically significant for blacks in 1970, however, and its size is small. A doubling of the AFDC payment increased the number of female heads by only 6 percent. Ross and Sawhill's study of female headship in low-income neighborhoods has also found positive and statistically significant impacts of AFDC payment level on blacks but not on whites.[2] Studies that use states rather than metropolitan areas as observations have found nonsignificant negative effects of higher AFDC payments on female headship.[3]

Analysis of data from the Panel Study of Income Dynamics (PSID) has also failed to produce conclusive results. Hoffman and Holmes found that in states with high benefit levels the dissolution rates of low-income couples rose from 3.8 percent to 10.6 percent.[4] This effect is substantially larger than those found by anyone else. Hoffman and Holmes' estimates of AFDC effects may be biased for the study suffers from a number of problems: the lack of a continuous measure of AFDC generosity, the absence of controls for regions or non-AFDC characteristics of the location, and the assignment of AFDC payment variables to couples that did not have children. The two other studies that used PSID data did not obtain significant coefficients on the variables measuring the generosity of AFDC.[5] Sawhill et al. found a small positive coefficient that implies that an extra $1,000 in AFDC benefits (in 1968 dollars) increased marital split rates about 6 percent. While five of the seven studies obtained positive coefficients on their AFDC payment variables, statistically significant effects were found in only three studies, and in two of these they were found for only one of the two racial groups studied. While it continues to seem logical (at least to economists) that a more generous AFDC program will increase the number of disrupted marriages, much more work (using new data sets) will have to be done before the proposition is proved.

Even if providing female-headed families with an adequate level of support does increase marital instability, it does not follow that "ending rules which prohibit assistance when the father of a family remains within the household . . . [will] keep families together."[6] There is no empirical support for this assertion. The best existing evidence suggests the opposite will occur.

In many states two-parent families with an unemployed head are already eligible for cash assistance from the AFDC-UP program. One of the purposes of this program is to reduce the incentive for families to split up in order to get AFDC. There is, however, no evidence that this program has reduced marital instability.

One way to examine the effect of AFDC-UP is to enter a dummy variable for the presence in the state of an AFDC-UP program in models predicting aggregate indicators of marital disruption. Since the number of families receiving AFDC-UP aid is small even in the most liberal state, a large impact is not to be expected. Since the restrictiveness of the local AFDC program's administrative and legal practices may also have direct impacts on the female headship rate, an unbiased estimate of the impact of an AFDC-UP program requires that there be a control for these practices. Using the welfare-recipiency rate among eligible female-headed families to control for these practices, Ross gets coefficients on the AFDC-UP dummy of $-.12$ ($t = 1.29$) for whites and $.00$ ($t = .06$) for blacks. Using a scoreboard of restrictiveness based on residency tests, wealth tests, and previous enforcement of man-in-house rules, Minarik and Goldfarb obtain a $.06$ ($t = 1.49$) coefficient. Controlling for divorce difficulty and an "employment rule," Honig obtains coefficients of $-.03$ ($t = .08$) for whites and $.15$ ($t = 2.94$) for blacks.[7] While the only statistically significant coefficient in the three studies is positive, the results taken as a whole are, as expected, inconclusive.

A study of the AFDC caseload in Alameda County, California, found that in every 3-month period about 5 percent of the two-parent families receiving AFDC-UP assistance break up.[8] These rates of dissolution (nearly 20 percent per year) are substantially higher than those experienced by two-parent, low-income families that are not on AFDC-UP. The yearly rates of dissolution in the control groups of the Income Maintenance Experiments were 4 percent in New Jersey and 5-10 percent for Seattle/Denver. The yearly dissolution rates for poor and near-poor couples in the PSID were 1.9 percent for whites and 3.0 percent for nonwhites.[9] Since the families that apply for AFDC-UP are not a random sample of all low-income families, these data do not prove that AFDC-UP caused the higher disruption rates. These results are, however, consistent with the findings of other research (to be presented shortly) that extending welfare to include two-parent families will increase rather than decrease marital instability.

Evidence from the Negative
Income-Tax Experiments

The best evidence about the likely effects on marital stability of extending cash assistance to two-parent families is provided by the negative income-tax experiments, where programs that are similar to the cash-assistance component of the Nixon Administration's Family Assistance Plan and the Carter Administration's 1977 Welfare Reform Plan were actually tried out, among families randomly assigned to experimental and control groups. If then statistically significant, nonartifactual differences are found between the experimental and control groups, it is possible to make the inference that being placed on the plan *caused* the difference. These experiments are better than any other kind of evidence, but they are not perfect. Ambiguities of interpretation may arise from small sample size, differential attrition of families from the experiment, and imperfect methods of measuring marital dissolutions. The families are promised only 3-5 years of payments and are studied only for that period of time. Consequently, predictions about the short- and long-term effects of a permanent program are necessarily extrapoliations.

Analyses of marital splitting are now available for all four experiments. In three of the four experiments the measured rates of marital dissolution were larger in the experimental group than the control group. For whites in the Seattle/Denver experiment, for instance, 13.6 percent of the control group and 18.5 percent of the experimental group's marriages had dissolved within 2 1/2 years, an increase of 36 percent. Among black families 19.1 percent of the control group and 27 percent of the experimental group's marriages had dissolved within 2 1/2 years, a 42-percent increase.

In the New Jersey experiment the ratio of the experimental-to-control split rate was .98 for whites, 1.66 for blacks, and 1.84 for Spanish speakers.[10] Figure 7-1 presents these unadjusted dissolution rates for each of the experiments. Table 7-1 presents coefficients on experimental dummies obtained in models that control for preexperimental characteristics of the family. For the low-payment plan the increases in marital split rates are statistically significant in both the New Jersey and Seattle/Denver experiments. They are not statistically significant in the Rural Income Maintenance Experiment because the low incidence of marital disruption in rural areas and the small sample size combined to produce only a limited number of splits to study. No increase in marital splitting occurred in the Gary experiment. The reasons for this contrast are discussed in the third section.

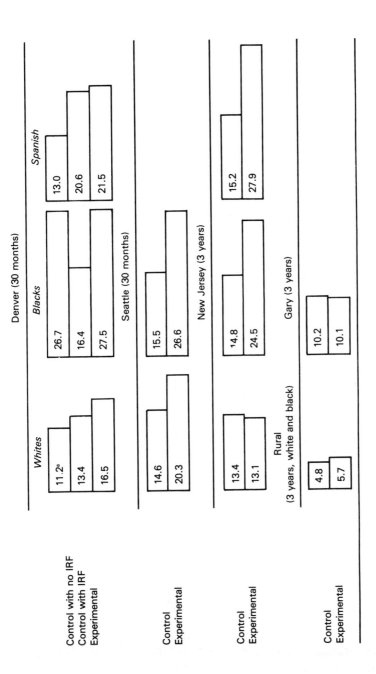

Figure 7-1. Unadjusted Marital-Dissolution Rates in the Negative Income-Tax Experiments

Source: HEW memos for Seattle/Denver and Gary, D. Wolf, ("Income in Labor Supply and Family Stability: An Empirical Analysis of Marital Dissolution," Ph.D. Dis. (University of Pennsylvania, University MicroFilms, 1977), for New Jersey, and R. Middleton and L. Haas, "Marital Dissolution and Family Interaction," chap. 8, in *Rural Income Maintenance Experiment: Final Report*, vol. 6, pt. 1, ed. D.W. Bawden and W.S. Harrar (Madison, Wisc.: Institute for Research on Poverty, University of Wisconsin—Madison, 1977, mimeographed.) for Rural. IRF means income report form. Since Experimentals were filing an IRF, the Denver control group that was filing an IRF is the better comparison group.

[a]Percentage splitting.

Table 7-1
Marital-Dissolution Rates across Experiments, Experimental Groups, and Plan Generosity, for a Three-Year Span

				Ratio of Experimental to Control Groups			
				New Jersey			
				Sawhill et al.,[c]	Knudsen et al.,[d]		
	Seattle-Denver[a]			1975	1977	Rural[e]	Gary[b]
	White	Black	Chicano				
Number of observations	1,297	939	535	968	968	616	643
Number of splits	166	179	81	116	116	36	63
Low-support plan	1.49[f]	1.47[f]	1.30	1.98[g]	1.79	3.00	.88
Medium-support plan	1.24	1.62[g]	.82	1.3	1.64	1.14	.72
High-support plan	.92	.94	.62	1.0	1.02	.85	

Note: Figures are based on models in which preexperimental characteristics of the family are controlled.

[a]Marital Dissolution equations estimated with the RATE model that contains control for: Normal Income (6 categories), city, log of marriage duration, wife's age, wife's education splined at 12 years, wife's wage, husband's age, husband's education, husband's wage, wife-husband wage ratio, number of children of different ages, family on AFDC prior to beginning of experiment. Memo to Douglas Wolf, HEW/ASPE, from Lyle Groenveld, SRI, October 25, 1973.

[b]These multipliers are unpublished RATE model estimates done by Douglas Wolf which control for age, education, number of children, labor-force status of both husband and wife, and the husband's hours of work.

[c]The multipliers for New Jersey combine the effects of support level dummies and the payment variable in the linear probability model of the full sample in table XII, p. 68, of I. Sawhill, G. Peabody, C. Jones, and S. Caldwell, *Income Transfers and Family Structure* (Washington, D.C.: The Urban Institute, 1975). Average weekly payments were $34, $15.30, and $7.70 for high-, medium-, and low-guarantee levels, respectively.

[d]The multipliers are derived from table 11.8 of J.H. Knudsen, R.A. Scott, and A.R. Shore's ["Changes in Household Composition," in *The New Jersey Income Maintenance Experiment*, ed. H.W. Watts and A. Rees, (New York: Academic Press, 1977)] analysis of transitions from nuclear to female headed status using 3 years of quarterly data from the New Jersey Experiment. The model used is the one that controls ethnic group and income prior to enrollment and ignores interaction between plan and ethnic group. Logit coefficients for no plan, low through high plans were −.318, .358, .256, and −.297, respectively.

[e]These multipliers are derived from the Adjusted Dissolution Rates given in table 1 of Middleton and Haas's analysis of the Rural Income Maintenance experiment. Linear-regression analysis was used to control for race, state, education, length of most recent job, 1969 family income, family size, welfare status at pre, farm occupation of head, age, nights in hospital, disability, net equity, and work at pre.

[f].10 > p > .05.

[g].05 > p > .01.

Why Marital Splitting Increased in the Experiments

The standard analysis of the marital-stability response to a universal cash-assistance program suggests that there should be two contrasting effects. The fact that the family is made better off while it remains together should reduce marital instability. This income effect, as it is called, should operate only for families that receive payments while intact and should be strongest in the most generous plans. The second effect results from the fact that the program also increases the income of one-parent families. By improving the financial situation of the wife if there is a split and reducing the need for child support, the program may induce some families to split. This "female-independence effect," as it is called, is also presumed to be the reason why women who work and earn good wages are more likely to dissolve their marriages. Evidence for the proposition that a female-independence effect is operating is provided by the rise in split rates of families on a NIT plan but earning too much to receive a payment (see row 3 and 4 of table 7-2). The only way families that are above the breakeven point can receive significant payments from the program is by reducing market work or splitting up. Splitting up seems to be one of the responses. It is also noteworthy that the increase in marital dissolution rates caused by the experiment is larger for families in which the wife was not working in the year prior to the experiment. As one would expect the independence effect of the NIT is larger for nonworking wives than for working wives.

Other aspects of the findings contradict standard theory, however. Standard theory predicts that families subject only to independence effects (that is, those above breakeven) should have higher split rates than those subject to counteracting income and independence effects (that is, those below breakeven). This is the case for Chicanos (compare lines 1 and 3 or 2 and 4 in table 7-2). It is not, however, the case for blacks, and the size of the difference for whites is negligible. For a female-headed family, the low-support plan is of roughly the same generosity as AFDC and food stamps combined (the payment option for controls who split). Families on the low-support plan are subject only to income effects, a fact that should by standard theory tend to lower the split rate. In fact, however, families on the low-support plan experienced statistically significant increases in marital split rates in two of the experiments (see table 7-1). Furthermore, couples on the least generous plans typically experienced larger increases in split rates than those on more generous plans. These contrasts between experimental findings and the predictions of a highly simplified standard theory suggest that some modification of the standard theory is in order.

The first possibility is that the experiment has a more powerful independence effect than the availability of an equivalent dollar amount from AFDC. Hannan et al. have suggested three reasons that this might occur.[11]

1. The transaction costs of applying for it are lower.

2a. Wives may feel that going on AFDC and food stamps carries more stigma than receiving payments from the experiments. (2b) If the experiment also produces a stigma, the two-parent family already receiving payments may have incurred these costs already so that splitting up may no longer produce an increase in stigma.

Table 7-2
Marital-Dissolution Rates in Seattle-Denver Experiment

Financial Status / Wife's Work Status in Preexperimental Period		Whites		Blacks		Chicanos	
		First[a] Events	All[b] Events	First Events	All Events	First Events	All Events
Ratio of experimental- to control-group split rates							
Below breakeven	Does not work	1.31	1.54	2.14	2.15	1.02	1.08
Below breakeven	Works	1.22	1.48	1.12	1.35	.90	1.13
Above breakeven	Does not work	1.57	1.58	1.33	1.19	2.19	1.64
Above breakeven	Works	1.38	1.39	.85	.85	1.12	.95
Ratio of working- to nonworking-wife split rates							
Both financials and controls		1.58	1.69	1.83	1.85	1.68	1.72
Number of cases		1,297	1,561	939	1,123	535	646

Source: Memo to Doug Wolfe, HEW/ASPE, from Lyle Groenveld, SRI, October 25, 1978.

Note: Controls include the assignment variables, age and education of husband and wife, duration of marriage, number of children, presence of a child under 10, and AFDC received the year before the experiment.

[a]First Events refers to the first split of marriages that were intact at enrollment.

[b]All Events includes in the analysis couples who became married after enrollment.

3a. Families on the experiment may have been more aware that if there were a split, the wife and children would be eligible for cash assistance and how much they would receive.

> Presumably some women with no welfare experience are unaware either of the fact they would be eligible for welfare were their marriage to end or of the levels of support available. . . . We took pains to explain that income-maintenance guarantees apply outside marriage.[12]

This information may substantially reduce the perceived costs of a marital separation. This information may "shock" the preexperimental equilibrium of an unfulfilling marriage and "focus attention on the current situation and heighten their sense of dissatisfaction."

3b. A second way in which the information environment of experimental families was different from controls was that they were actually on a plan and gaining real-life experience with its rules. Making monthly reports of income and receiving monthly checks (whose amounts vary inversely with the earnings of the primary worker) may quickly make family members "welfare wise." This experience with the high marginal tax rate may lead the family to consider sheltering the primary earner's income by having him split off from the rest of the family.

The NIT experiments might also have created male-independence effects.

4. Husbands in the control group may have feared the welfare department would pursue them for child support. The experiment, in contrast, made no effort to enforce child-support obligations. The contrast between current welfare programs and the experiments is even greater now, for there has recently been a federally financed intensification of efforts to obtain child support from disappearing fathers.

5. The small income-maintenance payment that splitting husbands were eligible for in three of the experiments may have produced a male-independence effect.

Independence effects (characteristics of the experiment that make the split state more attractive) are not, however, the only potential explanation of the increase in split rates of those on the low-support plan. A second potential modification of standard theory is to entertain the possibility that the receipt of income-maintenance payments may reduce the attractiveness of the married state.

6. It may lead to dissatisfaction with the husband's performance of his role. The role-performance interpretation asserts that most working- and middle-class families have traditional views about the role the husband is to perform. The husband is expected to be a breadwinner, and if he is not fulfilling his role, marital tension results. Robins et al. have found that the experiment increased the number and length of the head's spells of unemployment.[13] Friction produced by having the man around the house may build into a split.

In addition, the receipt of an income-tested transfer may be viewed by some families as a signal that the husband is a failure. In Bakke's words:

> Every goal he seeks to reach as a normal worker recedes further from realization when he turns to relief. Until that moment he could in a measure realize that even without current earnings the efforts he made in the past in the role of a "producer," a "good provider," a "good father" were still contributing to the support of his family. But now he has made a public declaration of his failure, and no rationalization can quite cover up the fact that a "reliefer" is not among the roles his associates respect.[14]

While the stigma attached to being on welfare has lessened, it may still be strong enough to induce some men to avoid this embarrassment by escaping from the situation altogether.

The evidence that is currently available does not allow one to choose between these alternatives. Here and there, however, there are fragments that count for or against particular explanations. Most of the explanations assert that eligibility for AFDC if a split occurs produces smaller female-independence effects than eligibility for an equivalent amount from the experiment. These explanations (nos. 1-4) would seem to imply that mothers who are eligible for more from AFDC than the experiment would choose to receive payments from the experiment rather than AFDC. In the New Jersey experiment, however, Garfinkel found that when AFDC payments exceeded experimental support, more than half of the splitting families chose to be on AFDC and not the experiment.[15] This suggests that at least some of the splitting women knew of AFDC and did not consider the extra transaction and stigma costs of AFDC sufficiently large to outweigh the small financial gain involved in being on AFDC.

Evidence for the possible importance of the stigma explanations (hypotheses 2a, 2b, and 6) is provided by the surprisingly low proportion of eligible two-parent families that apply for welfare. The Social Security Administration has estimated that half of the aged poor that are eligible for SSI fail to apply.[16] Studies by Coe and by McDonald have found that over three fifths of the two-parent families eligible for food stamps fail to apply.[17] Lidman has calculated that in 1971 only 15 percent of those categorically eligible for AFDC-UP were enrolled.[18] Boland has estimated that 523,000 families were eligible for AFDC-UP in 1970 compared to an average monthly caseload of 108,000 in that year.[19] The AFDC-UP program thus has a nonparticipation rate of 80 to 85 percent. In 1974 roughly half of poor families headed by a nonaged male reported that they received no transfers of any kind.[20] Outreach efforts have not been able to increase participation by significant amounts. These very low participation rates for two-parent families contrast with similarly calculated AFDC participation rates of 70 to 90 percent for female-headed families.

An analysis of participation in food stamps and of participation in SSI by the eligible aged supports the stigma explanation of low participation rates.[21] If ignorance of SSI or the strain of the applying were important, one would expect, ceteris paribus, social-security recipients and the better educated to have high rates of participation. If, however, the better educated internalize the norm of self-reliance more fully, one would expect more schooling to be associated with lower participation. Controlling for the dollar amount of SSI benefits available to the filing unit and a host of demographic characteristics, social-security recipients and the well-educated had lower rates of participation. The fact that individuals that are part of multiperson households (couples and eligible individuals living in the home of relatives) have lower participation rates for a given level of benefit also supports the stigma explanation. The perceived value of avoiding stigma should rise with wealth (the cost of obtaining information, on the other hand, depends on the value of the potential applicant's time, not wealth). Holding benefit level constant, there is a statistically significant tendency for the eligible aged who live with well-off relatives to have lower participation rates than those who live with less well-off relatives.[22]

The "signal of failure" (hypothesis 6) and "learning how the system works by becoming a recipient" (3b) explanations both apply only to families actually receiving payments while intact and are independent of how much the family receives. Income effects, in contrast, vary directly with plan generosity. As a result, it should be possible to distinguish between income effects that solidify marriages and the destabilizing "signaling" and "learning" effects.

The fact that split rates declined as the generosity of the plan increased suggests that, across plans, an income effect is operating.[23] Despite this decline, below-breakeven blacks have higher split rates than above-even blacks, and below-breakeven whites have essentially the same split rates as above-breakeven whites (see table 7-2)—a fact that suggests that receiving payments may have had both destabilizing and income effects, especially for blacks.

Other fragments of evidence supportive of the "signal of failure" hypothesis are the rise in psychological distress experienced by some experimental families even after the experiment had been underway for nearly two years and interactions of experimental status and background characteristics in the dissolution equations.[24] The proportionate increase in marital splitting seems to be greatest when the family's preexperiment earnings are low and when the wife is well educated and is able to command a good wage rate.[25] Families in which the husband's role performance is already threatened seem to be the ones most affected by being on the experiment.

So far the discussion has been directed to explaining why three of the negative income-tax experiments seem to have caused marital split rates to increase. The rates did not, however, rise in the Gary experiment. The reason seems to be that in some very important respects the administration of the Gary experiment was very different. In Gary the husband was the filer and the check was always made out to him. In the other experiments the check was made out to both the husband and wife, and cashing it required two signatures.

In the Gary experiment, neither the enrollment interview nor the explanation of program rules left with the families discussed what would happen if a marital split were to occur. Since the husband was a filer, a change of filer would be necessary if he left. The only mention of changing the filer in the program explanation given the family was, "The head may appoint someone else as filer (such as his wife) for the family unit by giving written consent allowing him or her to act as filer."[26] Some of the Gary families may have incorrectly thought they would lose eligibility if there were a split. The other experiments provided a much more complete description of the consequences of a split. Denver's short-form rules say, "If a person leaves the household, the income maintenance support guaranteed to the family will go down, but any income received by that individual will no longer be counted in the family basic income. Thus the total payment to the family may go down or up, depending on the income being received by the departing individual." The enrollers in the New Jersey experiment were instructed to say, "The family does not have to live together the way it is now—if someone in your family moves to another house the payment which you get will be divided up." The combination, in Gary, of making the checks out to the husband and not informing the families that a change in filer could be made easily if a split occurred seems to have created among the less well-informed participants a dependence effect, which counterbalanced the independence effects created among well-informed families.

The final difference is that during the first two years of the Gary experiment, the men who left their wives and families were not eligible for an income-maintenance payment. In the other experiments both the splitting male and, if he were to remarry, his new spouse and children were eligible for income-maintenance payments.[27] Thus the male-independence effects that were operating in the other experiments were not operating in the Gary experiment. In the Seattle/Denver experiment, however, male-independence effects do not seem to be important. If they were, we should have observed large numbers of splitting men receiving benefits from the experiment. Although attrition from the study meant that one was ineligible for payments, 51 percent of the splitting husbands for whom remarriage or reconciliation were not observed attrited. The fact that new wives and children become eligible for payments would seem to create strong incentives for splitting men to remarry. This does not seem to have happened, however, for the remarriage rate is not appreciably higher in the experimental group (18.6 percent) than in the control group (17.7 percent).[28]

In summary, the evidence available to date does not allow us definitively to reject any of the six proposed explanations of the unexpectedly high split rates in the low-support plans of the income-maintenance experiments. Perhaps to some degree all six are operating.

Policy Implications

A finding that universal cash assistance or increased unemployment will increase the rate at which marriages dissolve has policy implications only if society decides that such an outcome would be desirable or undesirable. Some might view splits caused by reduction in the stigma of being on AFDC or by greater awareness of opportunities for aid as giving the husband and wife the option to sever an already bad relationship. In this view, the experiments are not changing the basic quality of marital relationships; they are merely tipping a few of the worst marriages into the divorce court.

An alternative view is that the impact of the experiment is on marital interactions. The support payments for the wife if there is a split provide a convenient alternative to working out the problems that arise, and this may in some families lead one or both parties to reduce their investment in the relationship. Most marriages have their good times and their bad times, and adjusting to shocks requires effort and forbearance on the part of both husband and wife. If either the husband or wife stops making the effort to communicate his or her needs and to adjust to the changing needs of the other, their relationship will tend to deteriorate and may eventually dissolve. The evidence that is available to us now does not allow us to choose between these two views.[29]

The role-performance interpretation implies that in some families cash assistance disturbs a previously existing equilibrium and starts in motion a chain of events that leads to a dissolution. Some families will reject the notion that cash assistance is a sign of the husband's failure; others will respond to cash assistance by adopting a less traditional view of the husband's role in the family. Still other families will split apart.

The consequences for the children of an income-maintenance-induced separation are hard to assess. Holding constant race, family origin, and parents' education and occupation, the average child who grows up with only one of his natural parents spends roughly seven tenths of a year less in school and obtains jobs that pay about 10 percent less.[30] The experience of the marginal child may be different, however. It has been argued that a marital dissolution induced by reducing the stigma of AFDC will not hurt the children nearly as much as the averages quoted above. It might, in fact, help the children. Social science does not know the extent to which children are hurt by this type of marital split, and it is unlikely to be able to find out, for we will never do the controlled experiment that would be necessary.

While research into the process by which a split occurs and the consequences of a split for the children may inform the judgment, political decisions will ultimately depend primarily on the values of the relevant political actors.

For the rest of the chapter it will be assumed that the political system has set a goal in this area and that the goal is to minimize any marital side-effects of government policies that tend to destabilize marriages. It goes without saying that there will be occasions when achieving this goal conflicts with achieving other goals such as target efficiency, increasing GNP, and reducing the economic dependence of women.

The NIT experiment findings seem to imply that a reform of the welfare system should attempt to provide aid to low-income families in ways that are as unlike the experiments as possible. If the full responsibility for the increase in split rates in the low-support plans could be assigned to a particular hypothesis, the necessary modification of the NIT plans used in the experiments could be identified. To the extent that male-independence effects are crucial, the solution would be excluding able-bodied, single males from welfare eligibility. To the extent that the lack of child-support enforcement in the experiments was responsible, renewed efforts to enforce child-support obligations (not necessarily just for AFDC recipients) are indicated. If preferred explanation lies either in reduced transactions costs or greater knowledge that income support will be available for the family if a dissolution occurs (hypotheses 1 and 3), then segregating the programs that aid two-parent families from the ones that aid single-parent families is indicated. An earned-income tax credit, wage rate subsidies, targeted job credits and public jobs programs administered by IRS, Job Service, or CETA are alternative ways of accomplishing this.

There are two versions of the stigma explanation. If the key to experimental effects was a reduction in stigma costs suffered by female heads, we would seem to face a dilemma. There would appear to be no way to make single-parent families better off without creating more of them. The other version (2b) asserts that the key experimental effect was the increase in stigma costs suffered by the husband-wife families and the consequent reduction in the incremental stigma arising from the wife's receiving welfare after a split had occurred. This second version implies that two-parent families must be helped out in ways that do not stigmatize, even if it is less target efficient and more costly. If the role-performance explanation (hypothesis 6) is a major cause, aiding the family through jobs- and earnings-related transfers is the solution. The family must be helped in a way that does not signal the husband as a failure or create incentives for him to extend his periods of unemployment. The Gary experiment's results suggest that it might be important to make the check out to the husband rather than jointly to both.[31]

Given the uncertainty about the weight to be assigned to each of the six explanations, it would seem desirable to attempt to meet all six tests. The characteristics of such a program would seem to be:

1. It would limit the contact between two-parent families and the welfare bureaucracy.
2. Two-parent families would be made better off by reducing the amount of unemployment experienced by the head and/or by raising paychecks of the families' working members.
3. Where families with nonworking heads are aided, aid should be tied to past work effort of the head. Workmen's compensation, unemployment and disability insurance, and social security meet this test. AFDC, food stamps, and SSI do not.
4. Child-support obligations should be rigorously enforced.
5. It would give heads of families priority over single males in eligibility for targeted subsidies through private-sector employment and PSE jobs.
6. The family and its workers should not be stigmatized by participating in the program. They should not perceive themselves as receiving charity and where possible should not even be aware they have been helped.

Some of the policies that meet these tests focus on reducing the unemployment experienced by disadvantaged family heads; others concentrate on raising after-tax earnings of disadvantaged families. While such an approach to welfare reform should reduce the number of people on AFDC and SSI, it does not obviate the need for aiding families that lack able-bodied workers.

In general, any macroeconomic or structural policy that produces sustainable reductions in the unemployment of married family heads will have favorable side-effects on marital stability.[32] Policies that increase the unemployment rate of prime-aged males in order to gain a reduction in the aggregate unemployment rate are likely to have unfavorable side-effects on marital stability. Policies that promise sustainable reductions in everyone's unemployment—education and training, increases in competition or efficiency, TIPs or real wage insurance—are to be preferred. Targeting unemployment reductions on the heads of families that are most likely to disrupt—families headed by men with low wage rates or long periods of unemployment—will produce the largest reductions in marital stability. If, however, applying for a targeted job or job voucher is like applying for welfare (30-page application forms with rent receipts, pay stubs, and bank books to verify statements), a stigma may become attached to applying. If this occurs, few will apply and few employers will participate; the marital-stabilizing effect of any employment increase that does result will be reduced. The solution to this dilemma is to find subtle, nonstigmatizing ways of targeting. One promising approach is marginal wage subsidies for increases in hours worked. Such a subsidy lowers the cost of hiring low-wage workers proportionately more than it lowers the cost of hiring better-paid workers and thus shifts employment demand toward the less skilled.

Another approach would involve giving family heads priority in any queue that might develop for low-wage, public-sector jobs, and expanding the supply of such jobs. This was contemplated in the jobs component of the Carter Administration's 1977 welfare-reform proposal. Stigma can be minimized by integrating the PSE workers into the regular public-sector workforce and treating them no differently from other workers.[33] Alternatively, government might subsidize the private-sector employment of heads of low-income families. Unfortunately, the recently passed Targeted Jobs Credit, which offers firms a tax credit of up to $3,000 the first year and $1,500 the second year for hiring certain hard-to-employ workers, excludes from eligibility almost all family heads who are over age 25 and not on welfare.[34]

Lowering unemployment will not, however, bring large families headed by low-wage workers out of poverty. To support a five-person family at or above the poverty line, a full-time worker must earn more than $4.00 an hour. Yet in May 1978, 38 percent of all wage and salary jobs and 6 to 7 percent of the jobs held by prime-aged male heads of families were paid less than $4.00 an hour.[35] Even though poverty-threshold families pay almost no federal income tax, the other taxes they pay directly or indirectly—social security, sales, and property taxes—cumulate to over a third of their income.[36] The experiments seem to suggest that attempting to aid these families through welfare or an NIT risks disrupting their marriages.

A less disruptive form of aid would seem to be unobtrusive manipulations of the withholding tax to subsidize their earnings: either an earned-income tax credit (EITC) or a wage rate supplement (WRS). A 10-percent EITC of the first $5,000 of earnings of families with children is currently a part of the tax code. By raising the EITC rate, varying it according to family size, lengthening the accounting period, and increasing the marginal tax rate in cash and in-kind assistance programs, almost all the two-parent families that would have received cash-assistance payments under the Carter proposal could instead be receiving the same dollars of increased income in the form of a higher paycheck.[37]

A wage rate supplement is a government payment per hour of work over and above the standard wage for a job. To be eligible for a supplement, a job's standard wage would have to be equal to or greater than the minimum wage. There would be an upper limit on the number of hours of work that could be subsidized. (The limit would be somewhere between 180 and 210 hours per month.) In a WRS the per-hour payment is equal to some percentage (say, 50 percent) of the difference between a target wage (TW) and the worker's actual wage (W). The general formula is WRS payment = 0.5 $(TW - W)$ (hours worked). To take a simple example, a worker in a minimum-wage job (W = $2.90) who has a target wage of $4.90 would be eligible for a supplement of $1.00 an hour. If he works 160 hours in a month, he would receive $464 in normal wages and $160 extra [0.5(4.90 − 2.90) × 160] of wage supplement. If the worker were to obtain a job with a higher wage rate of $3.70, the supplement would fall to $.60 an hour. The worker's monthly supplement falls to $96, but his total earnings including the supplement rise from $624 to $688 ($96 + $592). Like the EITC, the WRS can be designated to integrate well with guarantee-type programs like food stamps, AFDC, and the cash-assistance component of the administration's welfare-reform proposal.[38]

A WRS has the advantage over an EITC of stimulating rather than decreasing work effort because it increases the monetary benefits of working longer hours. Like an NIT, a generous EITC places large numbers of moderate-income families on high marginal tax rates. Using the labor-supply function estimated for the Seattle/Denver experiment, Keeley et al. have calculated that, when added on top of the current set of income-maintenance programs, an NIT produces an earnings reduction of approximately one half the incremental cost of the program.[39] Garfinkel and Masters' simulations of labor-supply responses to NITs and generous EITCs imply that per dollar of cost, they produce similar reductions in labor supply.[40]

A wage rate supplement has a very different impact. If it is limited to primary earners, it will leave labor supply unchanged. Extending it to include wives will raise before-subsidy earnings by 10-20 percent of the amount paid out in supplements.

So far, all that has been claimed for earned-income tax credits and wage rate subsidies for families with children is that they can transfer an equal amount of income to a family with a working head without having marital-destabilizing effects as serious as welfare or cash assistance. The EITC and WRS raise the earnings of both single- and two-parent families. It is therefore conceivable that the female-independence effect arising from the improved circumstances of female-headed families would outweigh the income effect of raising the intact family's earnings and cause a net increase in marital instability.

Cross-sectional studies find that states and metropolitan areas with higher wage rates for women tend, ceteris paribus, to have higher rates of female headship. These same studies, however, find that a proportionate rise in both male and female wage rates is associated with fewer female-headed families. Holding the male-female wage ratio constant, Ross and Sawhill found that a 10-percent rise in the median income of intact families lowered rates of female headship in poverty areas of cities by 7 percent.[41] In the Minarik and Goldfarb study, a percent-in-poverty variable captures the effect of a general rise in wage rates.[42] Reductions in poverty reduce the incidence of female headship, though not to a statistically significant degree. Honig's regressions predict that for whites in 1970 and for both races in 1960 a general rise in wage rates will produce a reduction in rates of female headship.[43] If, as argued above, an EITC or WRS does not have the announcement, information, and stigma effects that welfare or an NIT seem to have, these studies suggest that general improvements in after-tax wage rates like those an EITC or WRS would produce would tend to lower rates of female headship.

This prediction must, however, remain tentative. An EITC or WRS increases the female-headed family's earnings by a larger percentage than it increases the earnings of the two-parent family. WRS limited to family heads leaves the wife's wage unchanged. EITCs tend to lower her after-tax wage. A fourth contrast between general shifts in wage levels and subsidy programs is that men who have left their families would lose eligibility. Current research does not allow us to calculate the net effect of all these influences with any degree of confidence.

Implications for Theory

Let us return to the implications of the NIT findings for theories of marital stability. The "economic" theories of marital instability that have been applied to the issues surrounding the design of income-maintenance programs have all made two crucial assumptions: (1) The impact of a transfer program on a family's welfare is a function of its impact on the family's income and leisure. Aside from the tendency of some programs (food stamps and housing allowances) to change consumption patterns, it has no other impact. (2) The wife has effective control over whether the family remains intact.

In light of NIT findings and other research, neither of these assumptions seems valid. There seems to be a need for a theory of why *men* marry and stay married and of how income-maintenance impacts upon their decisions that is complementary to the already developed female-oriented theories. What might such a theory look like? Let us start by listing some of the things a man gets out of marriage: (1) love—a stable love relationship; (2) children—his own children; (3) household services—cooking, cleaning, childrearing; (4) economies of scale in consumption and household production; (5) respect—the role of father and provider yields self-respect and the respect of others—family, peers, and the community.

The costs of marriage are: (1) time spent working to support the family, caring for children, and maintaining the quality of the relationship; (2) sharing of purchased goods and services; (3) sharing of power over how his time and the family's consumption goods are to be allocated.

The standard way to analyze the effect of income-maintenance programs on the attraction of marriage for a male is to focus on: (1) changes in the availability of purchased goods and services; (2) changes in the amount of time the husband has available for consumption or home production due to changes in the time he spends in the labor market. This perspective yields the unambiguous prediction that the availability of income maintenance to one- and two-parent families with children, but not to single men, should encourage unmarried men to marry and married men to stay married. From this perspective, the only aspects of the NIT experiments that would have caused men to want to dissolve their marriage were the experiments' lack of child-support enforcement (hypothesis 4) and the possible attraction of the small payment available to single men who earned less than $200 a month (hypothesis 5).

Time and financial resources are not the only things about a marriage that can be changed by income-maintenance programs. (1) They may induce a redistribution of family decision-making power away from the husband. (2) If becoming a recipient of income maintenance calls into question the husband's success as a provider, he may be accorded less respect by others, and he may lose self-respect as well. Both of these points reflect a role-performance perspective of marital instability. If income maintenance produces a redistribution of power, the husband's gains from marriage decrease while the wife's gains increase. The net effect on aggregate marital split rates is indeterminant. While one would expect that regardless of its direction, change would be disruptive of the preexisting marriage equilibrium, one cannot be sure overall split rates will rise. In contrast, the respect explanation produces the unambiguous prediction that receiving welfare lowers respect, and this in turn increases splits.

As currently constituted, however, the respect hypothesis has two deficiencies: (1) It does not explain why people desire respect nor why receiving welfare is not respected. Without such an explanation the hypothesis is open to the charge of being ad hoc. (2) It does not explain why the family would apply for welfare, if eventually it results in the husband losing so much respect that he chooses to leave his wife and children altogether.

Rather than taking people's views about what is respectable as given, we will derive them as predictions of a more general theory. People value the respect of others because they are taught to value it when they are children and because they are rewarded for behaving in a respectable manner when they are adults. The socialization process that produces these values is heavily influenced by groups like clan, tribe, church, school board, and nation that transcend the nuclear family. These groups directly control the institutions that do much of the socialization and indirectly influence the family's socialization activities. The social norms that are taught by this process reflect the interests of the larger group. Similarly, the social sanctions and rewards that continue to reinforce respectable behavior as an adult are under the control of the larger society. Major deviations from social norms are typically regulated by legislation with either loss of privileges, taxes, or court-imposed fines and incarceration as the ultimate sanction. An even more pervasive reinforcement for conforming to these norms is provided by the reactions of friends, neighbors, and coworkers.

The behaviors and traits that are taught and rewarded by this process are those that create benefits for other members of the community. The behaviors and traits that impose costs on others are discouraged by socialization and by expected negative reactions from others. A few examples will serve to illustrate the correlation between social norms and the social costs and benefits generated by a trait or act. Courage is respected especially by groups of fighting men and in cultures with a warring tradition. If there is to be a war, the nation or tribe involved in the war has a very powerful public interest in winning the war. Running away from the battle puts the remaining soldiers and the whole society in jeopardy. The group therefore has a powerful interest in instilling in the individual the traits that make for an effective fighting force—courage, discipline, and skill at arms.

A major element of socialization in almost every society is an attempt to internalize norms against lying, cheating, stealing, assault, and murder. Here again the public benefits are pervasive. The benefits of successfully internalizing these norms are not just the reduced risk of being robbed or assaulted and reduced expenditures on police: a major part of the benefit is the rights that can be awarded to people accused of crime and the privacy afforded the average citizen. Spendthrifts have always been derogated, especially by the bankers who have lent them money and the family members who must take on the responsibilities they do not or cannot perform. Further evidence for the correlation comes from the changes in what is considered socially acceptable behavior that are induced by the discovery that an act is damaging to others. When it was discovered that tuberculosis and other infectious diseases were transmitted by spitting, social norms about spitting started to change. What is common in all these examples is that the act of the individual is producing an externality—a benefit or loss experienced by other members of the larger group. Thus the primary function of social norms are the promotion of activities and traits that create positive externalities and the suppression of activities and traits that create negative externalities.

The externality theory of respect just outlined can be used to predict social norms regarding welfare dependency and the role of husbands and fathers. It predicts that there will be universal respect for the role of provider for one's family. It is in society's interest that fathers undertake and fulfill this responsibility, for otherwise society will have to provide transfers to the family and to take over a greater share of the job of socializing the family's children. The theory predicts that welfare recipients will be derogated, for while society may feel obligated to help the individual, it would prefer not to have to. Welfare is not a transaction in which society buys a service it would like to have more of. Rather it is a reaction to the guilt others feel when they see wretchedness and a response to a perceived threat to social stability if poor persons are allowed to reach the extremity of starvation.

The social norms that derogate welfare recipients have the behavioral objective of causing fewer people to become welfare recipients. Welfare recipients who are perceived to be able to support themselves if they would try—able-bodied single individuals and male family heads—are heavily stigmatized by being a welfare recipient. Welfare recipients who are not responsible for their helplessness—orphans and widows—are either not derogated or derogated in a much milder fashion.

The final issue that must be addressed is why, if the loss of respect will be so great as to cause some two-parent families to dissolve, does the family not turn down the option of going on welfare or the NIT? First, most two-parent families eligible for welfare do not, in fact, apply: Only 15 to 20 percent of AFDC-UP eligibles apply. In the New Jersey experiments 23 percent of the families contacted for a screening interview refused to be interviewed, 8 percent of those who submitted to the screening interview refused the preenrollment interview, and 8 percent of those offered an NIT payment chose not to participate. Early in the experiment when enrollment personnel were graduate students in economics, this refusal rate was especially high. Over the course of the 3-year experiment, attrition was 20 percent in the experimental group and 25 percent in the control group.

The reasons the refusals gave for not taking the money varied, but many reflected a sense of stigma. One was described as:

> He's a proud young man who finally insisted that he did not believe in taking money for nothing. He lived on what he himself alone, earned. He had a family and it was his responsibility, not anyone else's, to take care of them.[44]

The question remains, however, for those who did agree to participate and later found their marriages disrupted. There are a number of possibilities:

1. They saw that being a recipient would tend to be stigmatizing and would strain the marriage. They did not know the size of the effect, took a risk the effect would be small, and some lost.
2. The husband did not want to participate, but his wife did. Either she made the decision or he did not feel comfortable admitting to his reasons for not wanting the NIT. At least one husband seems to have sensed a conflict between himself and his wife on the issue when he said "His wife got him into this [by answering Urban Opinion Surveys] and he wants out."
3. They were misinformed. They were told the NIT experiment was not like welfare but later came to believe it was.
4. They made a mistake.

Concluding Reflections

For many years it was thought that one of the primary ways in which public policy might be designed to strengthen families was to expand eligibility for welfare benefits to include two-parent families. When this policy was implemented experimentally, we discovered that exactly the opposite happened. Two-parent families on a payment plan very similar in generosity to the cash-assistance proposal of the Carter Administration experienced marital dissolution rates that over a three-year period were 50 percent higher than the control group that was eligible for the current set of income-maintenance programs—food stamps, AFDC, and AFDC-UP. These findings, together with the extremely high split rates among Alameda County's AFDC-UP recipients, suggest that if strengthening marriages is an objective of public policy, expansions of welfare coverage to include two-parent families should be approached with real caution.

How then can government improve the financial circumstances of low-income two-parent families without stimulating marital breakups? The answer would seem to be to focus on jobs rather than cash assistance. Reflecting on why his marriage failed, a young man recently told a reporter "she lost respect for me as a man because I could not support us."[45] Nevertheless, he had turned down jobs saying, "I'm worth more than $2.90 an hour as a human being." A jobs strategy must simultaneously provide more jobs for the unskilled and drive up the wage rates for these jobs.

The optimistic interpretation of these findings is that the increase in marital instability was a unique response to one of the contrasts between the way the experiments and welfare are administered. The pessimistic interpretation derives from the fact that the NIT experiments are the first and only study of the response of two-parent families to welfare in which families were randomly assigned to treatment and control groups and in which the treatment group was well informed about the options open to them.

It is possible that if well-designed studies of the current set of income-maintenance programs (food stamps, SSI, AFDC-UP, unemployment insurance, disability insurance, and public service employment) were done, similar marital-destabilizing effects would be found. Selection bias and small sample size prevent the longitudinal data sets (Panel Study of Income Dynamics and National Longitudinal Survey) from providing definitive answers. If, however, recent improvements in methods of correcting for selection bias are applied to follow-up studies of accepted and rejected applicants for income maintenance, unbiased estimates of some of the marital-stability and labor-supply impacts of a program can be obtained. Such studies should receive high priority.

The reason that marital splits rates went up needs intensive examination. The effect of providing information about the availability of income maintenance can be examined by doing longitudinal studies of families contacted by welfare office outreach efforts. The consequences for the children of a divorce induced by income maintenance will be difficult to study, but they are so important that a major effort should be made.

Notes

1. M. Honig, "AFDC Income, Recipient Rates and Family Dissolution," *Journal of Human Resources* 9 (1974):303-323; M. Honig, "AFDC Income Rates and Family Dissolution: A Reply," *Journal of Human Resources* 11 (1976):250-260.

2. H. Ross and I. Sawhill, *Time of Transition: The Growth of Families Headed by Women* (Washington, D.C.: The Urban Institute, 1974).

3. J. Minarik and R. Goldfarb, "AFDC Income, Recipient Rates, and Family Dissolution: A Comment," *Journal of Human Resources* 11 (1976):243-249; M. MacDonald, *Food, Stamps, and Income Maintenance* (New York: Academic Press, 1977), pp. 104 and 146.

4. S. Hoffman and J. Holmes, "Husbands, Wives and Divorce," in *Five Thousand American Families: Patterns of Economic Progress*, vol. 4, ed. J. Morgan (Ann Arbor, Mich.: Survey Research Center, Institute for Social Research, University of Michigan, 1976).

5. I. Sawhill, G. Peabody, C. Jones, and S. Caldwell, *Income Transfers and Family Structure* (Washington, D.C.: The Urban Institute, 1975); D. Wolf, "Income in Labor Supply and Family Stability: An Empirical Analysis of Marital Dissolution," Ph.D. Dissertation, Department of Economics, University of Pennsylvania, University Microfilms, 1977.

6. *HEW News*, August 6, 1977.

7. Ross and Sawhill, *Time of Transition*; Minarik and Goldfarb, "AFDC Income, Recipient Rates, and Family Dissolution"; Honig, "AFDC Income, Recipient Rates, and Family Dissolution".

8. G. Silverman and M. Wiseman, "Family Fragmentation in the Aid to Families with Dependent Children Program." Paper presented at the meeting of the Western Economics Association, Berkeley, California. Welfare and Employment Study Project, Institute of Business and Economic Research, University of California, June 1979.

9. Adjusting for the higher split rates that are typical of California would not eliminate the discrepancy. The proportion of white 35- to 44-year-old, ever-married women who are separated or have at one time been divorced is 39 percent greater (.263/.189) in the San Francisco SMSA (which includes Alameda County) than it is nationally. For blacks, this proportion is 28 percent greater (.497/.388) than nationally. Raising the PSID four-year split rates by these percentage points would still leave the predicted yearly split rate for low-income couples at 2.6 percent for whites and 3.9 percent for nonwhites. About 44 percent of Silverman and Wiseman's AFDC-UP sample was black. See Silverman and Wiseman, "Family Fragmentation in the Aid to Families with Dependent Children Program."

10. Wolf, "Income in Labor Supply and Family Stability," p. 732.

11. M. Hannan, N. Tuma, and L. Groeneveld, "Income and Marital Events: Evidence from an Income Maintenance Experiment," *American Journal of Sociology* 82 (1977):1186-1211.

12. Ibid., p. 1208.

13. Philip K. Robins, Nancy B. Tuma, and K.E. Yeager, "Effects of the Seattle and Denver Income Maintenance Experiments on Changes in Employment Status" (Menlo Park, Calif.: Stanford Research Institute, April 1979, unpublished Paper).

14. W.E. Bakke, *Citizens Without Work* (New Haven: Conn.: Yale University Press, 1940), p. 255.

15. I. Garfinkel, "A Skeptical Note on the Optimality of Wage Subsidy Programs," *American Economic Review*, 1973.

16. Social Security Administration, Office of Research and Statistics, "Estimating the Number of People Eligible for the Supplement Securities Program," Staff Study, 1974.

17. R.D. Coe, *Participation in the Food Stamp Program Among the Poverty Population* (Ann Arbor, Mich.: Survey Research Center, Institute for Social Research, University of Michigan, 1977); MacDonald, *Food, Stamps, and Income Maintenance*.

18. R.M. Lidman, "Why is the Rate of Participation in the Unemployed Fathers Segment of Aid to Families with Dependent Children (AFDC-UF) So Low?" Institute for Research on Poverty, Discussion Paper 288-75, University of Wisconsin, Madison, Wisconsin, 1975.

19. B. Boland, "Participation in the Aid to Families with Dependent Children Families," U.S. Congressional Joint Economics Committee, Subcommittee on Fiscal Policy, *The Family Poverty Welfare Programs: Factors Influencing Family Instability*, Studies in Public Welfare, Paper No. 12, Part 1 (Washington, D.C.: Government Printing Office, 1973).

20. S. Danziger and R. Plotnick, *Has the War on Income Poverty Been Won* (New York: Academic Press, 1979).

21. M. MacDonald and I. Sawhill, "Welfare Policy and the Family," *Public Policy* 26 (1978):89-119; J. Warlick, "An Empirical Analysis of Participants in the Supplemental Security Income Program Among Aged Eligible Persons," Unpublished Ph.D. Dissertation, Department of Economics, University of Wisconsin, 1979.

22. Ibid.

23. There is a negative interaction between the families' normal income and the size of the marital splitting effect of income maintenance (see N. Tuma, M. Hannan, and L. Groeneveld, "Variation Over Time in the Impact of SIME/DIME on the Making and Breaking of Marriages," unpublished, SIME/DIME Research Memorandum Draft, Stanford Research Institute, February 1977, p. 12-15.) Since high-income families were more likely to be assigned to the more generous plans, the small response to the more generous plans reflects to some degree an effect of the assignment process. For median, normal-income families, some of which were assigned to all plans, a more generous plan seems to lower white and chicano split rates but increase black split rates.

24. P. Thoits and M. Hannan, "Income and Psychological Distress: Evidence from the Seattle and Denver Income Maintenance Experiments" (Stanford: Center for the Study of Welfare Policy Research, Stanford Research Institute, Memorandum 50, March 1978).

25. N. Tuma, L. Groeneveld, and M. Hannan, "First Dissolutions and Marriages: Impacts in 24 Months of the Seattle and Denver Income Maintenance Experiments" (Stanford: Center for the Study of Welfare Policy Research, Stanford Research Institute, Memorandum 35, 1976).

26. B. Tidwell, R. Kaluzny, E. Bruml, and D. DuRoss, "Participant's Knowledge and Understanding of the Gary Income Maintenance Experiments" (unpublished Paper, Princeton, N.J.: Mathematica Policy Research, 1977).

27. D. Kershaw and J. Fair, *The New Jersey Income Maintenance Experiment, Vol. 1: Operations, Surveys, and Administration* (New York: Academic Press, 1976), p. 87.

28. L. Groeneveld, M.T. Hannan, and N.B. Tuma, "Income Maintenance Impact on Remarriage of Males" (Menlo Park, Calif.: Stanford Research Institute, 1977, unpublished Paper).

29. Questions on marital happiness and adjustment were asked in the rural and Seattle/Denver income-maintenance experiments. Only the data from the rural experiment have been analyzed so far. R. Middleton and

L. Haas ["Marital Dissolution and Family Interaction," chap. 8 in *Rural Income Maintenance Experiment: Final Report*, vol. 6, part I, D.W. Bawden and W.S. Harrar, ed. (Madison, Wisc.: Institute for Research on Poverty, University of Wisconsin-Madison, mimeographed, 1977)] found no statistically significant association between being on the experiment and the mean changes of these scales. Income effects should improve marital adjustment while reduced investments in the relationship should worsen it, at least for a few of the families. The net effect of the experiment on the mean of these variables is indeterminate. If these scales do measure what they purport to measure, the reduced investment interpretation of the marital split results predicts that in the low- and medium-support groups there should be a few families that suffered a severe decline in marital adjustment and there should be a tendency for some of these families to split apart later. The "tipping the worst marriages" interpretation implies that in the experimental group there should be an especially strong tendency for the marriages with the worse marital adjustment at preenrollment to split apart.

30. D. Featherman and R. Hauser, *Opportunity and Change* (New York: Academic Press, 1978).

31. Currently most states give caseworkers discretion over whether AFDC-UP checks are made out to the father or mother. Checks are more likely to be made out to the mother when the father is considered unreliable or the marriage unstable. Karl Iario, in a personal communication, reports that, in Alameda County, California AFDC-UP families in which the mother receives the check are significantly more likely to split up than are families where the father is receiving the check. This finding could imply either that the caseworker's prophecy was accurate or that the prophecy becomes self-fulfilling.

32. One possible exception is a reduction in the generosity or eligibility for unemployment insurance. While the reduction in unemployment this would produce would stabilize marriages, the UI check (for which a man's past work efforts are responsible) continues to sustain the family, which may allow him to maintain the breadwinner role despite his unemployment. Lee Rainwater reports that "in families in which the husband receives disability payments, his status is as well-recognized as in families in which the husband is working." See L. Rainwater, "Crucible of Identity: The Negro Lower-class Family," *Daedalus* 95 (1966): p. 90.

33. The impressionistic studies of the depression years report that even though some considered a WPA job stigmatizing, unemployment was considered more so. Family heads who obtained WPA jobs regained much of their previously lost position in the family. It should be noted, however, that although WPA jobs were understood to be temporary, they did pay prevailing wages.

34. For a discussion of design issues, see J.H. Bishop and R. Haveman, "Targeted Employment Subsidies: Issues of Structure and Design," in *Creating Job Opportunities in the Private Sector* (Washington, D.C.: National Commission for Manpower Power, 1978).

35. See *Current Population Survey*, May 1978.

36. M. Reynolds and E. Smolensky, *Public Expenditure Tax and the Distribution of Income* (New York: Academic Press, 1977).

37. For a comprehensive description and analysis of Earned Income Tax Credits, see R. Haveman, "Work-conditioned Subsidies as an Income Maintenance Strategy: Issues of Program Structure and Integration," in *Studies of Public Welfare*, Paper No. 9 (Washington, D.C.: Government Printing Office, 1973).

38. How a wage rate supplement (WRS) would integrate with other income maintenance programs is discussed by R. Lerman, "JOIN: A Jobs and Income Program for American Families," in *Studies in Public Welfare*, Paper No. 19 (Washington, D.C.: Government Printing Office, 1974); J.H. Bishop and R. Lerman, "Wage Subsidies for Income Maintenance and Job Creation," in R. Taggert, ed., *Job Creation: What Works?* (Washington, D.C.: National Council on Employment Policy, 1977), pp. 39-70. The impact of a WRS on labor supply in both partial and general equilibrium models has been discussed in J. Kesselman, "Labor-supply Effects of Income, Income-Work and Wage Subsidies," *Journal of Human Resources* 4 (1969):275-292; J.H. Bishop, "The General Equilibrium Impact of Alternative Antipoverty Strategies: Income Maintenance, Training and Job Creation," *Industrial and Labor Relations Review* 2 (1979):205-223; I. Garfinkel and S. Masters, *Labor Supply Responses to Income Maintenance: Reassessment of the Cross-sectional Approach* (New York: Academic Press, 1977).

39. M. Keely, P. Robins, R.G. Spiegelman, and P. West, "The Labor Supply Effects and Costs of Alternative Negative Income Tax Programs," *Journal of Human Resources* 13 (1978): table 12.

40. Garfinkel and Masters, *Labor Supply Responses to Income Maintenance*.

41. Ross and Sawhill, *Time of Transition*.

42. Minarik and Goldfarb, "AFDC Income, Recipient Rates, and Family Dissolution."

43. Honig, "AFDC Income, Recipient Rates, and Family Dissolution;" and Honig, "AFDC Income, Recipient Rates, and Family Dissolution: A Reply."

44. Kershaw and Fair, *The New Jersey Income Maintenance Experiment.*

45. *The New York Times*, September 9, 1977.

8

Adolescent Pregnancy in the United States: An Evaluation of Recent Federal Action

Jacqueline R. Kasun

In the "Health Services and Centers Amendments of 1978" (Public Law 95-626, Titles VI, VII, VIII), the U.S. Congress found that "pregnancy and child-birth among adolescents . . . often results in severe adverse health, social, and economic consequences" and that, therefore, "Federal policy . . . should encourage the development of . . . health, education, and social services . . . in order to prevent unwanted early and repeat pregnancies. . . ." The act authorized $190 million to be spent over a three-year period on pregnancy testing, maternity counseling, "referral services," "family planning," "educational services in sexuality," and related services to pregnant and nonpregnant "adolescents."

Under the terms of the act these services would be provided through a national network of "public or nonprofit private" agencies established "in easily accesible locations" and supported by federal grants. The sums authorized in the act would constitute a net addition to several hundred millions of dollars authorized for the support of existing family-planning services that are open to all age groups, including adolescents.

The act represented the culmination of years of effort by such groups as Planned Parenthood, Zero Population Growth, the Population Council, and the Population Reference Bureau, as well as the Department of Health, Education and Welfare, to gain official recognition of the so-called teenage pregnancy epidemic. A flood of pamphlets, articles, and press releases had issued from these organizations in the years preceding passage of the act in much the same way that the so-called population explosion had been publicized a decade earlier. In the spring of 1978 the newly created Select Committee on Population held hearings and issued reports on "World Population: Myths and Realities," "Population and Development Assistance," "Legal and Illegal Immigration to the United States," and "Fertility and Contraception in America," giving three days' attention to "Adolescent and Pre-adolescent Pregnancy." The committee's report found adolescent pregnancy "alarming" and recommended strenuous federal action to combat it.

It is the contention of this chapter that the low and declining levels of adolescent pregnancy in the United States stand in surprising contrast to the conclusions reached by the committee and the action taken by Congress.

123

The chapter reviews these statistical facts, evaluating the major contentions in the committee's report and presenting some additional materials that bear upon the subject.

The fact that the statistical record of adolescent pregnancy provides little support for the alarm that pervades the committee's report or for the action that was taken by Congress suggests that other considerations may have prompted these responses. Examination of earlier statements on adolescent pregnancy by groups' having particular demographic objectives indicates that the reduction of adolescent pregnancy is seen as an important selective means of achieving low targeted rates of population growth. Recent federal action can be more readily understood in the light of this demographic objective than by referring to the statistical record of adolescent pregnancy.

Definition of Adolescence

The term "adolescence" is capable of elastic definition, depending on the purposes in hand. Webster defines "adolescence" as the "time of life between puberty and maturity" and an "adolescent" as a "person in his teens." Legally, individuals in our society arrive at maturity at different ages for different purposes. Physically, individuals arrive at maturity at widely differing ages.

Recent literature has discussed "adolescent pregnancy" as pregnancy occurring to women under 20 years of age. The term is relatively new, expressing a new concern. Much of the contemporary discussion of the subject has as its principal aim the instilling of the view that pregnancy among women under 20 is indeed a problem rather than merely a natural phenomenon among women who are arriving at physical maturity.

The Health Services and Centers Amendments of 1978 did not include in its six paragraphs of "Definitions" one for "adolescent," although the stated purpose of the act was to provide a wide range of new "services" for this class of individuals. The act does, however, define an "adolescent parent" to mean a "parent under the age of 21," a definition that expands the inclusiveness of the category of adolescence where parenthood is involved. Thus federal law now holds that persons who are parents do not emerge from adolescent immaturity until they are 21, one year later than the age commonly accepted for other persons.

It is probably unnecessary to point out that the term "adolescence" may, whenever convenient, be redefined to denote any period of preadult immaturity and dependence; and the age of entrance into adult responsibility and freedom can be set at any desired level, or even delayed indefinitely, if that is the policy makers' choice.

Statistical Facts

Figure 8-1 shows the large decline that has occurred in the birthrate among women under 20 in the past two decades. The official discussion, however, has managed to make it appear as if this decline had not occurred.

Beginning its discussion of "Trends in Adolescent Fertility" with the assertion, "There is perhaps no more serious health and welfare problem confronting the United States today than the high rate of adolescent pregnancy," the report of the House Select Committee on Population[1] is a most curious collection of conclusions that are contradicted by the accompanying evidence. Thus the report "supports" its opening assertion regarding the "high rate of adolescent fertility" with figures and a chart showing that during the past decade the birthrate to women under 20 in the United States has shown its steepest decline in history and has now arrived at one of the lowest levels ever to be recorded.

The report states:

Historically, the rate of teenage child-bearing increased sharply after World War II and peaked at 97.3 births per 1000 women of ages 15-19 in 1957. Since then, the rate of teenage fertility declined by 45 percent to reach a low of 53.5 births per 1000 women ages 15-19 in 1976.[2]

The report at this point provides a chart indicating that the birthrate to women aged 15-19 declined from a level of more than 60 per 1,000 in 1920 to slightly more than 50 in 1945, followed by the post-World War II increase and decline previously noted. The chart indicates that the 19-year decline from 1957 to 1976 brought the rate back to one of the lowest levels recorded.[3]

The report continues by noting that not only rates but numbers of births to women under 20 have been falling, despite a 58-percent increase between 1960 and 1976 in the number of "female teenagers." The report, nevertheless, avers that the number "has not decreased significantly," though the accompanying table shows a decline of 86,000, or 13 percent, between 1970 and 1976.[4]

Claiming that the "adverse health and social consequences of childbearing to teenage mothers are very different for girls who are at least eighteen or nineteen than for those who are younger," the statement continues by reporting that "(b)irth rates of women 18-19 years of age declined by 32.9 percent between 1966 and 1976," a rate that was "comparable to that of women ages 20-24 and 25-29 during the same period." The report, however, states that "the birth rates of teenage girls ages 15-17 declined by only 3.4 percent, while those of girls ages 10-14 actually *increased* by 33.3 percent between 1966 and 1976."[5] Two paragraphs later the report sheds a different

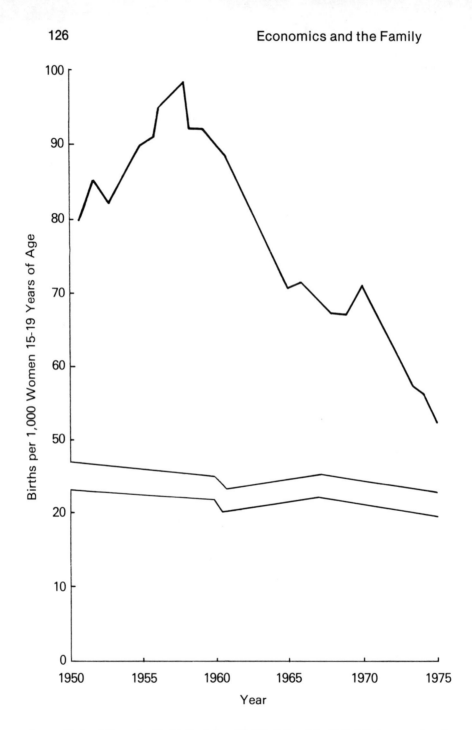

Source: National Center for Health Statistics, *Vital Statistics of the United States*, annual, and *Monthly Vital Statistics*.

Figure 8-1. Live Births per 1,000 Women 15-19 Years of Age, 1950-1976

light on these assertions by admitting that "the total number of births in this age category is still relatively small."[6] In fact, less than 4 out of 100 girls aged 15-17 and about 1 out of 1,000 girls under age 15 give birth in a typical year, and these rates have remained at approximately the same low levels for the past two decades. The very low birthrate for the youngest group varies on a year-to-year basis by as much as 20 percent, most of which must be regarded as random changes in a small number, having little statistical significance. It is arguable that these very low rates and small numbers represent some irreducible minimum of adolescent indiscretion that should not be expected to follow the trends for adults. Table 8-1 presents the rates by age groups for 1966, 1970, and 1976, and shows the much higher rates and larger reductions for the older group; it also shows the significant decline in *numbers* of births to this age group.

Nevertheless, having begun the discussion with the announcement that there is no more serious problem than adolescent pregnancy, the authors of the report are under some compunction to turn up evidence that this is so. This they attempt to do by reporting that nonwhite teenage fertility is higher than the corresponding rates for whites and that the rate of out-of-wedlock births for girls aged 15 to 19 "increased by 57 percent" between 1970 and 1976.[7] This latter statement is erroneous. There was an increase, but it was much smaller than this, perhaps amounting to as much as 7 percent, though this cannot be stated definitely since 12 states, including California, New York, and Ohio, have not required legitimacy status to be reported on birth certificates; also underregistration may have a selective effect on the reported numbers of out-of-wedlock births.[8] In both years the estimated

Table 8-1
Birth Rates, by Age of Mother, and Number of Births to Women Age 15-19, 1966, 1970, and 1976

Year	(1) Births per 1,000 Women 15-19	(2) Number of Births Women 15-19	(3) Births per 1,000 Women 18-19	(4) Births per 1,000 Girls 15-17	(5) Births per 1,000 Girls Under 15
1966	70.6	621,426	121.2	35.8	0.9
1970	68.3	644,708	114.7	38.8	1.2
1976	53.5	558,744	81.3	34.6	1.2
Percent of change, 1966-1976	−24.2%	−10.1%	−32.9%	−3.4%	+33.3%
Percent of change, 1970-1976	−21.7%	−13.3%	−29.1%	−10.8%	0

Sources: Derived from U.S. Department of Health, Education and Welfare, Public Health Service, National Center for Health Statistics, *Monthly Vital Statistics Report* for September 8, 1977, and March 29, 1978, and *Vital Statistics of the United States*, annual.

numbers and rates of out-of-wedlock births to teenagers are small, amounting to about 2 births for every 100 unmarried women under the age of 20.

Table 8-2 presents the data, showing the rather small increase in the number of births per 1,000 unmarried teenagers and the much larger increase in the *proportion* of total births that are occurring out-of-wedlock to this age group. This latter development reflects the fact, of course, that birthrates to married teenagers have fallen so steeply while those to unmarried teenagers have risen somewhat.

It thus appears that although young mothers are having fewer babies, they are having a somewhat larger proportion of them outside of marriage. There are other indications that marriage is declining even more precipitately than childbearing among the young. Rising proportions of both sexes have never married. For example, in 1960, 76 percent of all 18-year-old females had never been married; by 1975 this proportion had risen to 84 percent.[9]

The committee's report discusses trends in births to women under 20 but does not discuss trends in pregnancies including abortions. Two persons, however—Dr. Wendy Baldwin and I—submitted testimony to the committee on this point. Dr. Baldwin concluded that, even if it is assumed that there were *no* abortions in 1960 as compared with an estimated 283,000 in 1974, the adolescent pregnancy rate would nevertheless have declined by 4 percent between the two years. On the other hand, on the assumption of equal abortion ratios in the two years, she found that the teenage pregnancy rate declined 36 percent between the two years.[10]

In my investigation I assumed no abortions in 1955 and an estimated

Table 8-2
Estimated Live Births Out-of-Wedlock per 1,000 Unmarried Women 15-19, and as a Proportion of all Births to Women 15-19, 1970 and 1976

Year	Estimated Live Births Out-of-Wedlock per 1,000 Unmarried Women, 15-19	Estimated Live Births Out-of-Wedlock as a Percent of All Births to Women, 15-19
1970	22.4	29%
1976	24.0	40%
Percent of change, 1970-1976	+7.1%	+37.9%

Source: Derived from U.S. Department of Health, Education and Welfare, Public Health Service, National Center for Health Statistics, *Monthly Vital Statistics Reports*, September 8, 1977, and March 29, 1978. See text for discussion of the problems of estimating out-of-wedlock births.

294,000 on adolescents in 1974; estimating that each abortion replaces between .45 and .89 live births (to allow for repeat abortions and the fact that it is physically possible for women to have abortions more frequently than they can give birth), I found that the adolescent birthrate would in the absence of abortion at most have remained the same in 1974 as in 1955 or have fallen by 13 percent.[11]

In response to a request in 1978 by Senator Alan Cranston, the Department of Health, Education and Welfare studied 1971-1976 trends in pregnancy and births among women 15-19 years of age and found that the adolescent pregnancy rate, including pregnancies terminated by induced abortion, increased only 1.2 percent during the period. This very small change may not be statistically significant in view of the difficulties involved in estimating the number of illegal abortions in 1970. The results of this study are reproduced in table 8-3 and show the very large increases in legal abortions as well as the large decreases in fertility and the rather small change in the pregnancy rate.

The committee noted with concern that "(s)ome sociologists, such as Kristin Luker, argue that the easy availability of abortions may have encouraged men and women to be less careful about using contraceptives,"[12] but were assured by one witness that he could find "no support for Luker's speculations."[13] In fact, Luker's study was a careful analysis of the decisions made by a large number of women seeking abortions, and she found that a significant proportion who knew about contraceptives had discontinued their use in an apparent decision to risk pregnancy, given the "back-up" availability of abortion.[14]

Given that some women use legal abortion as their form of "birth control" and that it is physically possible to have abortions more frequently than children, the statistical effect of abortion should be to increase the incidence of pregnancy, at least among younger women who are experiencing lower pregnancy orders and will therefore be affected by the sterility *sequelae* of abortion only after a delay. The delayed sterility effects of abortion may be expected subsequently to depress the incidence of pregnancy among older groups.

Moving right along in its quest for evidence of crisis, the committee report begins its discussion of "Health and Social Consequences" by asserting, "Most experts agree that early child-bearing can be harmful to both the mother and child." This brave beginning continues rather lamely, however, with the admission that "(i)t seems likely . . . that maternal mortality rates for teenagers are no longer considerably higher than for older women" since 1976 data showed rates for teenagers actually lower than for women in their early twenties, the period traditionally regarded as having lowest rates.[15]

Table 8-3
Comparison of Fertility Rates and Pregnancy Rates for All Women 15-19 and Sexually Active Women 15-19, from 1971 to 1976

Year	Number of Women 15-19[a]	Number and Percent Sexually Active[b]		Number of Births[c]	Number of Abortions[d]	Number of Fetal Deaths[e]	Number of Pregnancies[f]	Fertility Rate 15-19[g]	Fertility Rate Sexually Active[h]	Pregnancy Rate 15-19[i]	Pregnancy Rate Sexually Active[j]
1971	9,712,000	2,923,312	(30.1%)	627,942	158,376	9,625	795,943	64.7	214.8	81.95	272.3
1972	9,936,000	3,209,328	(32.3%)	616,280	191,284	8,206	815,770	62.0	192.0	82.10	254.2
1973	10,120,000	3,481,280	(34.4%)	604,096	201,377	7,791	813,264	59.7	173.5	80.36	230.7
1974	10,253,000	3,752,598	(36.6%)	595,449	237,294	7,399	840,142	58.1	158.7	81.94	223.9
1975	10,345,000	4,003,515	(38.7%)	582,238	266,714	6,756	855,708	56.3	145.4	82.72	213.7
1976	10,443,000	4,271,187	(40.9%)	558,744	301,372	6,309	866,425	53.5	130.8	82.96	202.9
Percent of Change, 1971-1976	+7.5%	+46.1%	(+35.9%)	−11.0%	+90.3%	−34.5%	+8.9%	−17.3%	−39.1%	+1.2%	−25.4%

Source: Reproduced from letter to Senator Alan Cranston from Henry Aaron, Assistant Secretary for Planning and Evaluation, Department of Health, Education and Welfare, dated August 18, 1978, copy provided by Senator Cranston to Jacqueline Kasun.

[a]From Bureau of the Census, midyear estimates.

[b]From Kantner and Zelnik, *Family Planning Perspectives*, January-February, 1978. Assumes linear increase between 1971 and 1976.

[c]From NCHS, natality statistics.

[d]From CDC, abortion surveillance data. Number abortions for 1976 estimated.

[e]From NCHS, registered fetal deaths of 20 or more weeks gestation. Excludes induced abortions.

[f]Estimated number of pregnancies based on births, abortions, and fetal deaths. Number *underestimates* actual number of pregnancies as fetal deaths prior to 20 weeks are not reported.

[g]Live births per 1,000 women age 15-19.

[h]Live births per 1,000 sexually active women age 15-19.

[i]Pregnancies per 1,000 women age 15-19.

[j]Pregnancies per 1,000 sexually active women age 15-19.

The report continues by saying that one 1960 study found higher rates of infant mortality among babies born to girls under 15.[16] This was highly selective reporting of the testimony that had been presented by witnesses before the committee. In fact, the committee had received testimony that there is little evidence of elevated health risks either to younger mothers or to their children.[17] Recent studies conducted at the University of Rochester School of Medicine have found that pregnancy is no more risky for teenagers than for women in their twenties. The Rochester Adolescent Maternity Project studied predominantly black, innercity teenagers with an average age at delivery of 16 years.[18] The physicians Semmens and Lamers, studying a large number of teenage pregnancies, found that "complications are rare," and that the incidence of prenatal death of the baby is only a fraction as high as in the general population.[19]

In a major survey of existing research on "Parental Age as a Factor in Pregnancy Outcome," published in 1974 by the Population Council, it was noted that the age of 18 is apparently the best age to have a child and that the risks to both mother and baby are probably somehat higher, though not necessarily serious, at other ages.[20] All studies have found that the younger the mother, the less likely she is to have a baby with Down's syndrome (mongoloid mental retardation).[21] Figures from Denmark and from Indian reservations in the United States, in both of which health care is freely available to all age groups, show death rates for infants born to teenage mothers lower than among babies of older mothers.[22] It has long been observed that the incidence of breast cancer is lowest among women who have had a first child while under the age of 20.[23]

Figures indicating special health difficulties for adolescent mothers and/or their babies probably chiefly reflect the unequal access to health care on the part of lower-income groups. For example, one study of teenage childbearing that concluded that the babies of mothers under 20 have higher risks of "prematurity, mortality, and serious physical or intellectual impairment," corrected its data for income differences in only one table; and in that one table, showing rates of low birth weights by age and income of mother, the teenage mothers had lower percentages of low-birth-weight infants than did older mothers with the same income.[24] In general, low-income women had higher percentages of low-birth-weight infants than did higher income women.[25] In her textbook *Adolescent Obstetrics and Gynecology*, Dorothy Hollingsworth states, "The single most important factor determining a favorable or unfavorable pregnancy outcome is the economic level of the patient and her family."[26]

Though the committee's report asserts that "(t)here are indications that child abuse is more prevalent among young mothers than among older mothers,"[27] in 689 pages of testimony by 24 expert witnesses over a period of three days, no evidence was submitted that this is so. Other major investigations have similarly failed to find evidence of greater child abuse by teenage parents than by older parents. For example, in a Kentucky study of adolescent mothers, "almost all mothers appeared warm and loving . . . and none was felt to be hostile and negative."[28]

Though the committee claims that "(p)regnancy is the single most common cause of school drop-out among young girls,"[29] it received testimony that two thirds of the girls who drop out of school do so for reasons other than pregnancy.[30]

The committee's report expresses alarm over "unwanted" births to teenage mothers[31] but gives no figures on how many there might be of these, other than to point out that teenage mothers now keep 90 percent of their babies born out-of-wedlock, despite the large unsatisfied demand for adoptable children.[32] Throughout its report, the committee uses interchangeably the terms "unwanted," "unplanned," "unintended," "born out-of-wedlock," and even "conceived out-of-wedlock." These semantic manipulations, which have been criticized in public hearings on population topics for at least the past eight years,[33] enable the writers of the report to convey the impression that most young mothers would prefer to be rid of their children and that the crusade to stamp out "unwanted" births is of crucial importance to the national welfare. In the same spirit of obfuscation, Congress provides no definition of "unwanted" in its act aimed at "preventing unwanted . . . pregnancies among adolescents."[34]

Similarly, though the committee report repeatedly expresses alarm over the "very high" incidence of adolescent pregnancy[35] and Congress pledges itself to try to reduce this rate, there is no explanation of what "high" means in this context. As already shown, the *birthrate* among women under 20 is in fact about half as high as it was 20 years ago. The *numbers* of births to this age group have been declining since 1970 and can be expected to decline still more substantially in coming years since the number of women in this age group will fall by 19 percent, or almost 2 million persons, in the decade of the 1980s. Witnesses before the committee had offered conflicting testimony as to whether U.S. birthrates among teenagers are high when compared with other countries. On the one hand, Planned Parenthood submitted a graph[36] comparing births to women under 20 in several countries, most of which had higher rates than the United States. In making this comparison, however, Planned Parenthood simply left all but 3 of the more than 30 countries with rates higher than the United States off the graph![37] The committee received testimony that, in fact, on a scale of all adolescent birthrates for which United Nations estimates are available, the United States stands in the lower one third.[38]

Once again it appears that, as in the case of Humpty Dumpty's conversation with Alice, words mean whatever their users want them to mean. Furthermore, without any definition of what "high" means, it will be impossible ever to decide when determined national action has brought these rates of childbearing to levels that are sufficiently "low." The programs to curb adolescent pregnancy are therefore inherently openended and subject to whatever definitions and goals may be espoused by the ruling bureaucracy.

The committee reported with alarm that "in 1976 the Federal Government disbursed nearly half ($4.65 billion) of the total AFDC appropriation to households with women who were teenagers when they first gave birth."[39] The fact that these women might have required public assistance regardless of the age at which they began childbearing was not mentioned in the report. Indeed, one witness had submitted evidence that early childbearing is *not* directly related to the probability of being a welfare recipient.[40] Nor did the report mention the fact brought out in testimony that the great majority of teenage mothers—an estimated two thirds—do *not* become welfare clients[41] nor that the majority of public-assistance recipients become self-supporting within a few years, often within a few months.[42] Also not mentioned was the fact that Aid to Families with Dependent Children (AFDC) is one of the relatively small public-transfer programs, accounting directly for only 2 percent of all public expenditures, and for no more than a probable 4 percent when allowance is made for the addition of food stamps, health care, and housing allowances.[43]

Neither the committee nor any of its witnesses addressed the question of the *net* effect that adolescent pregnancy is presently having, or can be expected to have, on public-assistance expenditures. To answer this question, it is necessary to take into account on an annual basis not only how many new young mothers are joining the public-assistance rolls but also how many teenage welfare mothers of previous years are becoming self-supporting.

Using U.S. vital statistics, estimates of welfare dependency presented by witnesses to the committee, and national data on the length of time during which families remain dependent on public assistance, it is possible to make estimates of these net effects. The majority of public-assistance recipients have no more than two children and have received assistance for three years or less.[44] Based on data presented to the committee by Dr. Kristin Moore, it can be estimated that 33 percent of teenage mothers receive AFDC support for some time after birth.[45] This implies the equivalent of 87 percent of all young women giving birth out of wedlock. (This estimate can be used for statistical purposes even though some young mothers receiving public assistance are married women.)

Using this figure, it can be estimated that 193,650 new mothers—with their babies a total of 387,300 persons—joined the welfare rolls in 1975, as shown in table 8-4. This would cause a 3-percent gross increase in total AFDC dependency and costs, a figure that is surprisingly small in view of

Table 8-4

Number of Births to Women Age 15-19, Estimated Births Out-of-Wedlock, and Estimated Net Change in AFDC Rolls, 1975 and 1980

Year	(1) Number of Births to Women 15-19[a]	(2) Out-of-Wedlock Births[b]	(3) Teenage Mothers and Babies Added to AFDC[c]	(4) Teenage Mothers and Children Leaving AFDC[d]	(5) Net Change in AFDC (Col. 3-Col. 4)
1975	582,238	222,600	387,300	315,100	72,200
1980	450,700	225,300	392,000	382,200	9,800

Source: Adapted from U.S. Social and Rehabilitation Service, *Findings of the 1973 AFDC Study*, June, 1974, reprinted in *U.S. Statistical Abstract 1977*, p. 350.

[a]1975 figure from U.S. National Center for Health Statistics; 1980 figure estimated from U.S. Bureau of the Census projection of number of women aged 15-19 and projection of 1970-1976 straight-line trend in birthrates to women 15-19.

[b]1975 figure from U.S. National Center for Health Statistics; 1980 figure equals number of births to women 15-19 times projection of 1970-1976 semilogarithmic trend in proportion of births out-of-wedlock.

[c].87 × (column 2) × 2.

[d]Based on number of years as recipient:

	Percent of Recipients
Under 1 year	27.7
1-3 years	27.3
4-5 years	18.8
6-10 years	27.3

the fuss being made over the "soaring welfare costs" supposedly resulting from the "teenage-pregnancy epidemic." Moreover, it is too large a figure because it is gross and does not take account of the teenage mothers of previous years who are now becoming self-supporting and leaving the AFDC rolls. Using figures on average duration of welfare dependency, it is possible to estimate how many teenage welfare mothers of previous years became self-supporting in 1975. This estimate is 315,100 mothers and children; the 1975 net addition was therefore 72,200, which amounted to 6/10 of 1 percent of the total number of persons receiving AFDC in that year. This estimate takes into account the much-decried increase in "illegitimacy" among teenagers and shows that its net effect on total AFDC dependency in 1975 was very small.

The net increase in AFDC caused by new teenage mothers in 1975 would amount to less than $60 million. Allowing for their proportionate share of Medicaid, food stamps, and housing assistance, the total increase would amount to perhaps $120 million.[46]

By projecting the declining present trend in birthrates among teenage mothers, the declining numbers of women in this age group, and the rising proportion of births occurring out of wedlock and assuming, as before, that 87 percent of new unmarried teenage mothers go on welfare and that duration of dependency is distributed as in the previous estimate, it is possible to make a forecast for 1980. In that year, as shown in table 8-4, 392,000 new teenage mothers and babies can be expected to become dependent on public assistance, while 382,200 would become self-supporting, for a net gain of 9,800, which would amount to less than 9/100 of 1 percent of 1975 AFDC rolls or $8 million. If public-assistance rolls are larger in 1980 than in 1975, this net increase would constitute an even smaller percentage of the larger total.

What these comparisons mean is that teenage childbearing is presently making a very small net contribution to welfare dependency and, at present rates of change in the relevant variables, within a few years will be making a trivial contribution, if any. The reason for the projected decline, of course, is that the numbers of births to this age group are falling, even though the proportion of births taking place out of wedlock may be increasing. The point of this discussion is to put the facts into appropriate perspective, as has not been done in the rhetoric of crisis with its emphasis on the "soaring welfare costs" that supposedly result from the "epidemic" of teenage pregnancies.

In contrast to the small and declining net contribution of teenage childbearing to welfare dependency, the costs of public family-planning services can be expected to continue to increase explosively. Over the five-year period beginning in 1973, these expenditures approximately tripled to a 1978 annual amount estimated at $359 million.[47] Over the decade 1967-1977, they increased eighteenfold.[48]

To deal with the so-called adolescent pregnancy problem, the administration requested for fiscal year 1979 an increase of $142 million,[49] which would bring the annual domestic expenditure to a level of $500 million approximately. In addition, an amount between $150 million and $200 million would be allocated to population control in American foreign-aid programs.[50] At current rates of increase, family planning will be a multi-*billion*-dollar public program within the next decade.

Subsequent to the committee hearings and the passage of PL 95-626, a highly publicized report on the costs of teenage childbirth was issued by SRI International.[51] This study concluded that the present discounted value of the 20-year public costs associated with births to teenage mothers in 1979 amounted to $8.3 billion. In order to arrive at this enormous total, the report made a number of unrealistic assumptions, the most important of which was that not only do teenage mothers and their babies receive public assistance but so do the mothers' husbands in large numbers and over long periods of time. In fact, however, such husbands rarely qualify for public-assistance payments; indeed, marriage typically disqualifies the woman for public assistance.[52] The report also includes as part of the costs of a teenage birth large welfare expenditures assumed to be paid to subsequent children of the same mother. The report assumes that women continue to receive large public-assistance benefits for 20 years after a teenage birth when, in fact, the available data indicate that such long periods of welfare dependency are extremely rare.[53] In addition, the study used unrealistically high estimates of per-capita public-assistance costs including large allowances for extraordinary medical costs supposedly caused by births to young mothers and unexplained large allowances for "social-service expenditure(s)" on their behalf. The net result is gross overstatement of the public costs associated with teenage childbirth.

To summarize, in 1976 out of 100 young American women aged 15-19, about 5 gave birth. This represented a decline of almost half since 1957, when about 10 out of 100 in this age group gave birth. The rate for 1976 was one of the lowest ever to be recorded. The majority of these young mothers in 1976—3 out of 5—were married women beginning their families in the usual way. About 2 out of 100 young *unmarried* women aged 15-19 gave birth in 1976; this was substantially the same rate as in 1970. The proportion of births occurring out of wedlock increased, and legal abortions among women under 20 have increased greatly. It appears that births to women under 20 would have declined in recent decades even in the absence of legalized abortion. Further substantial declines in numbers of births to teenagers can be expected in the future as the number of young women in the 15-19 year age group declines by 19 percent in the decade of the 1980s. Claims of special health problems among mothers under 20 and their children prove to have been exaggerated and seem mainly to reflect unequal access to health care. The net contribution made by teenage mothers to public-assistance rolls is small. Other problems supposedly created by the so-called teenage pregnancy crisis appear also to have been exaggerated.

It therefore appears that the conclusions reached by the House Select Committee on Population and by the Congress—that major new public interventions are necessary to reduce pregnancy among women under 20—seem to flow more from official preconceptions than from the evidence. In a word, the committee's report and Public Law 95-626 have been written in the same spirit of population alarmism that has infused public policy making since the mid-1960s. In order to understand the development of these preconceptions with respect to adolescent pregnancy, it is instructive to examine some earlier documents dealing with the topic.

Previous Statements on Adolescent Pregnancy

Adolescent pregnancy received official attention as early as 1969, when President Nixon's Commission on Population Growth and the American

Future authorized several research reports on the topic.[54] The reports covered the topics now accepted as standard—statistical trends, "medical aspects," "illegitimacy," "unwanted" pregnancies, and "genetic implications." The reports encountered the usual difficulties in separating the effects of age from the effects of income and in defining terms and getting reliable data. They noted the lack of reliable data on births out of wedlock.[55] The statistical results failed to indicate any special difficulties for teenage parenthood that could not be explained by low income. In fact, as previously noted, where no income differences existed, teenage mothers were shown to have a lower proportion of low-birth-weight infants than mothers over age 20.[56] It can be argued, of course, that a justification for public attempts to reduce teenage pregnancy is that teenage mothers are likely to be poor. It is equally arguable that the facts, if they sugggest any public action at all, more clearly justify programs to improve economic opportunity and access to health care than attempts to reduce births among a particular age group who are likely to be poor. Indeed, the latter has overtones of being a "final solution" to the poverty problem.

One of the most interesting findings noted in the research reports was that comprehensive public birth-control programs (of the type to be provided under PL 95-626) do not reduce illegitimacy. One of the reports compared illegitimacy trends in several areas having large public birth-control programs with the trends in areas having few such programs. While illegitimacy declined in all areas studied, it did so most dramatically in the areas having few public birth-control "services."[57]

The research reports, however, had a more pressing interest than merely reducing illegitimacy or the percentage of low-birth-weight infants. They pointed out that the size of the population could be significantly reduced by eliminating all births to teenage mothers.[58] The commission accordingly "deplore(d) the various consequences of teenage pregnancy" and recommended that "birth control information and services" and public sex education be provided to teenagers.[59] It also recommended that all restrictions on voluntary sterilization be eliminated[60] and that "abortions . . . be performed on request" at public expense.[61]

The idea that the size of the population could be reduced by eliminating births to women under age 20 again appears in the Nortman study previously mentioned.[62] The introduction to this study states that the idea for it had come from Bernard Berelson, then president of the Population Council, who devoted his Annual Report of 1971 to the topic "18-35 in place of 15-45?" and in her final paragraphs Nortman discusses Berelson's seminal idea—the "Demographic Implications of Eliminating Births at Ages of Reproductive Inefficiency." She asks, "Suppose, then, that women were to reproduce only during the 15-year period from age 20 through age 34," rather than during the 30-year period from age 15-44 heretofore regarded as the years of normal female fertility. Using estimates from various countries as to numbers of births by age of mother, she calculates that this 15-year shortening of the childbearing period for the world's women would reduce the world population growth rate from its 1970 level of 20 to about 13 per 1,000 population per year. "The impact of this," she says, "can be seen in the fact that, at a growth rate of 20 per thousand per year, the population doubles in 35 years compared with 53 years at a rate of 13 per thousand per year."[63] She ends by saying that "the means by which to restrict fertility to ages 20-34 are beyond the scope of this paper" but that a successful program of this type "would . . . bring relief to a world coping with growth rates that retard economic development and threaten nature's ecological balance."[64]

Two years after the publication of the Nortman study, the Alan Guttmacher Institute, which is the "Research and Development Division" of the Planned Parenthood Federation of America, gave a new thrust to the effort by launching its public-relations campaign against the so-called teenage pregnancy epidemic. The campaign began with the publication of the institute's pamphlet *11 Million Teenagers: What Can Be Done About the Epidemic of Adolescent Pregnancies in the United States.*[65] The pamphlet, which decried the so-called epidemic in dramatic terms, was widely distributed to, and subsequently quoted by, leaders in Congress and in television broadcasting, newspaper publishing, parent-teachers organizations, churches, youth organizations, and other creators of public opinion. The pamphlet *11 Million Teenagers* is reproduced in toto in the Hearings of the Select Committee.[66] Many of its statements and its dramatic headlines were quoted not only in the report of the Select Committee on Population but in countless letters to the editor and reports to community groups through the nation—"U.S. Teenage Childbearing Rates are among the World's Highest," "11 Million Teenagers are Sexually Active," "One Million Teenagers Become Pregnant Each Year," and so forth.

Having thus sounded the alarm, the Guttmacher Institute published in the following year a plan for action, entitled *Planned Births, the Future of the Family and the Quality of American Life: Towards a Comprehensive National Policy and Program.* Sponsors of the plan included not only Planned Parenthood itself but also Zero Population Growth, the Population Section of the American Public Health Association, and other family-planning organizations. The plan proposed "a high priority national program of services, education and research related to fertility, and *a shift in public policy to one which supports the regulation of fertility as a universal service* (emphasis added), with government prepared to intervene to assist those who are disadvantaged for any reason in obtaining the services they need and want. . . ."[67] The plan thus called for a considerably more emphatic public commitment to "fertility regulation" than had heretofore existed;[68] and it did not specify that this "universal service" should be provided only to voluntary recipients. The plan expressed special concerns regarding pregnancy among "women younger than age 20" because so many of these pregnancies are "unintended."[69] The plan therefore gave high priority to "new initiatives" "to reduce . . . the number of unintended pregnancies and births among teenagers,"[70] and it called for the establishment of a "national network for early detection of pregnancy," "school-based education programs," "community information and outreach programs," and programs to "(e)ncourage hospitals to provide abortion services."[71] In order to launch this all-out attack on "unintended fertility,"[72] the plan called for "immediate attention from the Administration and Congressional leadership"[73] and 1979 federal spending of $410 million on domestic family planning, increasing to $783 million by 1981.[74]

"Immediate attention" was, indeed, as we have seen, forthcoming from the administration and Congress, with authorized expenditures exceeding the amounts requested by Planned Parenthood. Not only was the president of the Guttmacher Institute a prominent witness before the Select Committee on Population[75] but other witnesses also called for a national network of "pregnancy-detection centers"[76] in order to prevent both first births and "recidivism"[77] (that is, additional births) among women under 20.

That the select committee was animated by demographic concerns is suggested in its question, "Is the right of parents to determine the number of children they will have an absolute one? Is it unethical to restrict population size through legislative action? What is compulsion?"[78] Numerous witnesses had expressed to the committee not only demographic but eugenic concerns as well, in their discussions of adolescent pregnancy. Sargent Shriver, for example, spoke of "this Committee's interest in improving the quality of life and enhancing the biological product of this society, rather than just controlling or limiting births."[79]

True, in its Letter of Transmittal the committee assures the speaker of the house that its report on fertility and contraception merely "reviews the methods, means, and services available to help American men and women achieve their family size goals."[80] The report makes it clear, however, that the committee believes the government has the duty to influence those "family size goals" in major ways, by distributing "public service messages concerning . . . family planning and its medical and socioeconomic advantages,"[81] by "(m)easures to increase the acceptability of . . . contraceptives,"[82] by "further research on motivation,"[83] by "(f)urther effort . . . to investigate more acceptable fertility regulation for adolescent males and females . . . and for women over 35,"[84] by devoting more resources to the "urgent need for contraceptive services among rural women,"[85] by supporting "outreach activities to attract males to these [contraceptive] services,"[86] and by evaluating "sterilization regulations to protect individuals from undergoing this procedure without careful consideration, with the goal of ensuring that these regulations do not hinder voluntary and informed access to this procedure,"[87] as well as in other ways.

Clearly, the committee saw a large public responsibility for intervention in the area of individual fertility regulation. It is equally clear that the committee intends that the weight of U.S. policy shall be on the side of discouraging childbearing. This must be regarded as a significant statement of public intent in an area of decision making that has heretofore been regarded as personal.

Public Law 95-626, which was passed substantially as submitted by the Department of Health, Education and Welfare to the select committee,[88] provides for the requested national "network" of pregnancy-detection centers with their accompanying "services." In my county applicants for grants under the new legislation were preparing their requests as the law was being considered, and if the money is granted, our county health department will begin this year to operate such centers, offering comprehensive "screening," "counseling," and "referral services" at three local high schools.[89] The magnitude and intensity of the effort to be made in this county can be judged by the fact that a $50,000-a-year program is planned for a high school that has 1,000 students.

Evaluation of Recent Federal Action

This chapter has shown that the statistical facts regarding adolescent pregnancy do not support the major conclusions reached by the Select Committee on Population, nor do they justify the actions taken by Congress. These conclusions and actions can be understood, however, in the light of demographic objectives that have been held for a number of years by influential public and private groups. To those committed to the cause of reducing or eliminating population growth, the youngest groups of potential parents—lacking confidence, experience, and money—have appeared as a natural target for public action. By stimulating concern, through a well-organized campaign carried out over a period of years, for the supposedly very special problems of these younger groups, the advocates of population control have achieved one of their major objectives: explicit public commitment to the reduction of pregnancy.[90]

In evaluating recent federal action regarding adolescent pregnancy, it cannot be argued that the new program is entirely undesirable. If it succeeds in providing young mothers with good medical care or in other ways compensating for the disadvantages of poverty that to some extent differentially affect young parents and their children, much good may be accomplished.

It should be noted in this connection, however, that the etiology of poverty and teenage pregnancy and the relationship between these two phenomena are far from clear. Poor women do begin childbearing at relatively early ages, but whether this is a cause or a result of their poverty, or neither, is unclear.

Nor can it be confidently predicted that public pressure on these women to delay their childbearing will significantly improve their economic and social circumstances. Not every young woman is a latent entrant into a higher income bracket provided only that she remains childless. Moreover, the publicly funded services provided by the act may not supplement and strengthen but tend to discredit and weaken the traditional source of assistance to adolescents and inexperienced young mothers and fathers—their own parents. By offering young people "comprehensive" birth-control and other social services under conditions of "confidentiality," the new bureaucracy of tax-supported teenage-pregnancy experts may take the republic still further along the path of replacing the family with public agencies.

But this is not all that the new program signifies. Unlike previous family-planning legislation, which merely attempted to make "voluntary family planning services readily available to all persons desiring such services,"[91] PL 95-626 has the explicitly stated objective of reducing pregnancy. The new program thus takes the nation a giant step forward in the direction of comprehensive public intervention in fertility regulation and population control.

It thus raises profound questions of social philosophy that are beyond the scope of this chapter but deserve scholarly attention. To what degree and on what grounds is government justified in intervening in personal fertility decisions? Do some births impose sufficient costs on society that society is justified in attempting to prevent those births? Or are most of the costs of children born by their parents who may therefore be trusted to make rational decisions on their own behalf? Do our concepts of human dignity require that government abstain from intervention in such areas of personal decision making except to protect individual lives or property?

The extant literature on adolescent pregnancy has neither distinguished nor discussed these considerations. Most of it muddles the personal costs of childbearing with the social costs, and none of it has given consideration to the offsetting personal and social value of the new human lives in question. It therefore fails to come to grips with the underlying welfare issues.[92] It may be that, in the coming years, as the full effects of current low fertility rates maintained over a long period of time become more obvious, these welfare qustions will receive more adequate attention.

Notes

1. *Report* of the Select Committee on Population, U.S. House of Representatives, 95th Cong., 2nd sess., "Fertility and Contraception in the United States" (Washington, D.C.: Government Printing Office, 1978), p. 57.

2. Ibid.

3. Ibid., p. 58. Data on births by age are affected by the fact that birth registrations were not collected for the entire United States until 1933, as well as by underregistrations in the covered areas since then. These factors have some unknown effect on levels and long-term trends in births by age of mother. There is no doubt, however, that a major decline has taken place since the late 1950s. See U.S. Department of Health, Education and Welfare, Public Health Service, National Center for Health Statistics, *Vital Statistics of the United States*, 1973, vol. 1, Natality, Technical Appendix.

4. *Report* of the Select Committee on Population, p. 58.

5. Ibid., p. 59.

6. Ibid.

7. Ibid., p. 61.

8. See U.S. DHEW, *Vital Statistics of the U.S.*, 1973; also Phillips Cutright, "Illegitimacy in the United States: 1920-1968," Commission on Population Growth and the American Future, *Research Reports*, vol. 1 (Washington, D.C.: Government Printing Office, 1972), pp. 429-433.

9. U.S. Bureau of the Census, *Current Population Reports*, Series P-20, no. 287.

10. *Hearings* before the Select Committee on Population, "Fertility and Contraception in America: Adolescent and Pre-adolescent Pregnancy," 95th Cong., 2nd sess., vol. 2, (Washington, D.C.: Government Printing Office, 1978), p. 245.

11. *Hearings* before the Select Committee on Population, p. 309.

12. Ibid.

13. Ibid.

14. Kristin Luker, "Contraceptive Risk-Taking and Abortion: Results and Implications of a San Francisco Bay Area Study," *Studies in Family Planning*, vol. 8, no. 8, August 1977.

15. *Report* of the Select Committee on Population, p. 62.

16. Ibid., pp. 62-63.

17. *Hearings* before the Select Committee on Population, pp. 307-308, 391-392.

18. Elizabeth R. McAnarney, M.D., et al., "Obstetric, Neonatal and Psychosocial Outcome of Pregnant Adolescents," prepublication manuscript presented in part at the American Public Health Association meetings, Miami, Florida, October 21, 1976.

19. James P. Semmens, M.D., and William M. Lamers, Jr., M.D., *Teen-age Pregnancy* (Springfield: Charles C. Thomas, 1968), pp. 86, 93.

20. Dorothy Nortman, "Parental Age as a Factor in Pregnancy Outcome and Child Development," The Population Council: *Reports on Population/Family Planning*, no. 16, August 1974.

21. Ibid.

22. Ibid., p. 33.

23. W.P.D. Logan, "Cancer of the Female Breast: International Mortality Trends," *World Health Statistics Report* 28:232-251, World Health Organization, 1975.

24. Jane A. Menken, "Teenage Childbearing: Its Medical Aspects and Implications for the United States Population," Commission on Population Growth and the American Future, *Research Reports*, vol. 1, (Washington, D.C.: Government Printing Office, 1972), p. 349.

25. Ibid.

26. A. Karen Kessler Kreutner, M.D., and Dorothy Reycroft Hollingsworth, M.D., eds., *Adolescent Obstetrics and Gynecology* (Chicago: Yearbook Medical Publishers, 1978), p. 121.

27. *Report* of the Select Committee on Population, p. 65.

28. Kreutner and Hollingsworth, *Adolescent Obstetics and Gynecology*, p. 270.

29. *Report* of the Select Committee on Population, p. 63.

30. *Hearings* of the Select Committee on Population, p. 34.

31. *Report* of the Select Committee on Population, p. 19.

32. Ibid., p. 64.

33. Juan Ryan, Statement, Hearing before the Subcommittee on Public Health and Welfare of the Committee on Interstate and Foreign Commerce, "Family Planning Services," 91st Cong., House of Representatives, 2nd sess., Serial No. 91-70 (Washington, D.C.: Government Printing Office, 1970), pp. 448-453.

34. See Public Law 95-626, Sec. 602.

35. See *Report* of the Select Committee on Population, pp. iii, 57, 65.

36. *Hearings* before the Select Committee on Population, p. 556.

37. Jacqueline R. Kasun, Statement, in *Hearings* before the Subcommittee on Public Health and Welfare, p. 310.

38. Ibid.

39. *Report* of the Select Committee on Population, p. 63.

40. Kristin A. Moore, *Hearings* before the Select Committee on Population, p. 289.

41. *Hearings* before the Select Committee on Population, p. 295.

42. U.S. Bureau of the Census, *Statistical Abstract of the United States: 1978*, 99th ed. (Washington, D.C.: Government Printing Office, 1978), p. 350.

43. Based on *Economic Report of the President, 1978* (Washington, D.C.: Government Printing Office, 1978), p. 222.

44. U.S. Bureau of the Census, *Statistical Abstract of the United States: 1977*, 98th ed. (Washington, D.C.: Government Printing Office, 1977), p. 350.

45. *Hearings* before the Select Committee on Population, p. 295, table 5.

46. Derived from table 4 and *Economic Report of the President, 1976* (Washington, D.C.: Government Printing Office, 1976), p. 94, and *Economic Report of the President, 1978* (Washington, D.C.: Government Printing Office, 1978), p. 222.

47. According to Sargent Shriver in *Hearings* before the Select Committee on Population, p. 177.

48. Based on *World Population Growth and Response* (Washington, D.C.: Population Reference Bureau, April 1976), p. 189, and *Planned Births: the Future of the Family and the Quality of American Life* (Planned Parenthood et al., June 1977), p. 15.

49. *Report* of the Select Committee on Population, p. 89.

50. U.S. House of Representatives Select Committee on Population, *Newsletter*, January 25, 1979, p. 3.

51. SRI International, *An Analysis of Government Expenditures Consequent on Teenage Childbirth*, SRI Project 8173, prepared by John C. Robbins for Stacey Jordan, Project Director.

52. See U.S. Department of Health, Education, and Welfare, *Characteristics of State Plans for Aid to Families with Dependent Children* (Washington, D.C., 1976) and *Statistical Abstract of the United States: 1977* 98th ed. (Washington, D.C.: Government Printing Office, 1977), p. 350.

53. *Statistical Abstract of the United States: 1977* 98th ed. (Washington, D.C.: Government Printing Office, 1977), p. 350.

54. Commission on Population Growth and the American Future, *Research Reports*, vol. 1 (Washington, D.C.: Government Printing Office, 1972).

55. Ibid., pp. 429-433.

56. See Menken, "Teenage Childbearing."

57. Commission on Population Growth and the American Future, *Research Reports*, pp. 419-421.

58. Ibid., p. 350.

59. Ibid., pp. 189-190.

60. Ibid., p. 171.

61. Ibid., p. 178.

62. Nortman, "Parental Age as a Factor in Pregnancy Outcome."

63. Ibid., p. 49.

64. Ibid.

65. Alan Guttmacher Institute, *11 Million Teenagers: What Can Be Done about the Epidemic of Adolescent Pregnancies in the United States* (New York: Planned Parenthood Federation of America, 1976).

66. *Hearings* before the Select Committee on Population, pp. 553-613.

67. *Planned Births: The Future of the Family and the Quality of American Life* (Planned Parenthood et al., June 1977), p. 2.

68. Ibid., p. 17.

69. Ibid., p. 8.

70. Ibid., p. 3.

71. Ibid., table 1, pp. 18-19.

72. Ibid., p. 8.

73. Ibid., p. 30.

74. Ibid., pp. 26-28.

75. *Hearings* before the Select Committee on Population, pp. 170-177.

76. Ibid., p. 169.

77. Ibid., p. 163.

78. Select Committee on Population, Report, "World Population: Myths and Realities," U.S. House of Representatives, 95th Cong., 2nd sess. (Washington, D.C.: Government Printing Office, 1978), p. 7.

79. *Hearings* before the Select Committee on Population, p. 178.

80. *Report* of the Select Committee on Population, p. iii.

81. Ibid., p. 11.

82. Ibid., p. 17.

83. Ibid.

84. Ibid., pp. 16-17.

85. Ibid., p. 11.

86. Ibid.

87. Ibid.

88. *Hearings* before the Select Committee on Population, pp. 154-158.

89. Humboldt County Health Department, Application for Grant to Provide Adolescent Health Care, dated December 22, 1978.

90. See *World Population Growth and Response* (Washington, D.C.: Population Reference Bureau, April 1976), pp. 191-192; see also *Hearings*, "Family Planning Services," 1970, pp. 230-233, 235, 254-255, 457, *inter alia*.

91. Public Law 91-572, Sec. 2(1).

92. For a valuable discussion of the welfare issues raised by childbearing and public population control, see Julian L. Simon, *The Economics of Population Growth* (Princeton: Princeton University Press, 1977), especially chap. 18.

Increasing the Economic Self-Sufficiency of Teenage Mothers

Steven Paul Schinke,
Lewayne Dorman Gilchrist,
and Thomas Edward Smith

The current epidemic of teenage pregnancy in this country has yielded an alarming set of health, social, and economic statistics. Pregnant teenagers and their babies suffer significantly more health and developmental problems than do older mothers and their babies.[1] Compared to couples who have delayed childbearing until they were past age 20, teenage parents experience more marital difficulties and higher divorce rates.[2] They also appear at risk for child abuse and neglect.[3] Research with teenage parents documents significant self-recrimination, low self-esteem, depression, and—particularly for women—disruption and painful change in relationships with the nuclear family.[4] Suicide attempts are especially high among pregnant teenagers.[5] Pregnancy is a common reason for dropping out of high school and lost years of education are rarely made up.[6] Lacking marketable skills, teenage parents face high unemployment;[7] employed adolescent mothers and fathers are much more likely to hold low-prestige positions, express greater job dissatisfaction, and earn lower incomes than their nonparent peers.[8]

Certainly, economic problems that adolescent mothers face are among the most serious and pervasive of all untoward consequences of early childbearing. Teenage mothers are over twice as likely to fall below federal poverty lines than women who become mothers when they are 20 or older.[9] Recent data indicated that 91 percent of a large sample of women giving birth at ages 15-19 had neither full- nor part-time employment 19 months after delivery.[10] It is hardly surprising that 55 percent of teenage mothers receive public assistance—3.3 times the percentage of mothers first delivering at ages 20-23.[11] In 1975 half the total AFDC expenditure of $9.4 billion went to households of women who bore first children while teenagers.[12] Economic self-sufficiency thus is essential for millions of U.S. teenage

Research reported in this chapter was supported in part by Maternal and Child Health Services Project 913 from the Bureau of Community Health Services (Health Services Administration) and by National Institute of Child Health and Human Development Grants HD 02274 and HD 11095 (National Institute of Health), all administered through U.S. Public Health Service, Department of Health, Education, and Welfare and awarded to the University of Washington Child Development and Mental Retardation Center.

147

mothers as more of them keep their babies and government resources become less available.[13]

This chapter presents results from a study addressing a crucial first step in increasing teenage mothers' self-sufficiency: ability to apply competitively for employment. Choice of the target step was guided by extensive experience with programs for teenage mothers[14] and by a body of empirical literature documenting that young people—especially racial minority-group members—do not know how to present themselves effectively when applying for jobs.[15] Such lack of skill represents a major barrier to employment. A local school-age parent continuation program requesting assistance in upgrading vocational guidance services was the study setting.

Methodology

Setting and Participants

Housed in a public school, the continuation program was charged with providing educational, social, and vocational services to teenage mothers and expectant mothers. Few young women planned on furthering their education beyond high school. Program staff, teachers, and students therefore gave high priority to need for remunerative employment. Study participants were 46 mothers or mothers-to-be enrolled in the school-continuation program. Selection criteria were willingness to participate and signed consent forms from parents or legal guardians and from each student. Ages ranged from 13 to 19, with a mean age of 16.73, and standard deviation (*SD*) of .51. Educational levels ranged from eighth to twelfth grade, with a mean grade level of 19.77 (*SD* = 1.08). Ethnic backgrounds were primarily racial minority: 40 young mothers were black, three were white, two were Hispanic, and one was a Native American. Most participants had one or more children, with a mean age for all children of 8.29 months (*SD* = 7.03); 12 participants were pregnant at the time of the study.

Assessment

To quantify employment-application skill deficits, participants completed an assessment battery including:

Nowicki-Strickland Locus-of-Control Scale. This measure, associated with perceptions of self-esteem and self-concept,[16] was chosen because past research has shown minority youths "characterized by a passive presentation of self."[17]

Multiple-Affect Adjective Check List (MAACL). Following procedures suggested by Zuckerman and Lubin, the MAACL was given shortly before a simulated job interview to assess performance anxiety.[18]

Employment Application Form. Each young mother completed an employment application asking closed-ended questions on demographic, academic, and previous employment history, and openended questions on criminal convictions, outstanding debts, and health. Employment applications were scored by two personnel specialists responsible for hiring and job placement. Specialists scored all applications using Likert scales to quantify attributes of neatness, competence, academic qualifications, employment history, and recommendation for hiring/placement. Expressed as a Pearson product-moment correlation coefficient (r), agreement between the two specialists was .796 (SD = .128).

Videotaped Job Interview. After completing the employment application, young women were individually videotaped in a simulated job interview. Over a 10-minute period, an interviewer asked each participant about her educational and employment background, career goals, and general personality characteristics. Interviews were scored by four raters quantifying nonverbal skills of eye contact and smiles and verbal skills of positive self-statements, negative self-statements, unspecific responses, and non-responses. Raters took absolute frequency counts for all skills except eye contact, scored as total seconds of eye contact with the interviewer. Computation of interrater agreement yielded a mean r of .921 (SD = .086).

To facilitate a comprehensive overview of assessment data, mean scores on all measures are presented in table 9-1. Since differences associated with age and previous work experience were of interest, subdivisions by these categories are also given. Sample sizes varied due to missing data.

Locus-of-Control Scale. Data yielded by the 40-item questionnaire showed an overall mean of 12.767. This compares with normative means ranging from 12.01 to 12.98 for samples of tenth-, eleventh-, and twelfth-grade students.[19] Age differences on the measure were not significant, $X^2(1)$ = .123, $p < .75$, nor were differences between participants who had held jobs and those who had not, $X^2(1)$ = .000, $p < .95$.

Affect Adjective Check List. Results on this measure showed an overall mean of 2.619, compared with 6.700 for 100 adult females who completed the checklist prior to a job interview.[20] Young women showed no differences when grouped by age, $X^2(1)$ = .592, $p < .50$, or by previous employment, $X^2(1)$ = .043, $p < .90$.

Table 9-1
Pretest Mean Scores Categorized by Age and Previous Work Experience

Assessment Measure	All Participants (N = 46)	Age Category		Previous Work Experience	
		13-16 (n = 20)	17-19 (n = 24)	None (n = 18)	Some[a] (n = 26)
Locus-of-control scale[b]	12.767	13.444	12.217	12.765	12.752
Affect adjective check list[c]	2.619	1.667	3.000	2.313	2.650
Employment application[d]					
Neatness	5.250	5.250	5.250	5.429	4.577
Competence	5.438	5.625	5.250	5.429	5.024
Academic qualifications	5.125	4.750	5.500	5.429	4.874
Employment history	3.125	4.250	2.000	1.857	3.989
Recommend hiring/placement	6.938	8.375	5.500	7.286	6.209
Job interview[e]					
Eye contact	.488	.488	.513	.516	.483
Smiles	.703	.876	.552	.768	.682
Positive self-statements	1.338	1.287	1.361	1.423	1.321
Negative self-statements	.796	.665	.884	.849	.780
Unspecific responses	.384	.339	.411	.404	.380
Single-word responses	.396	.442	.347	.397	.406
Inappropriate responses	.031	.044	.023	.015	.044
Nonresponses	.065	.130	.017	.117	.035

Note: *n*s are unequal due to missing data.
[a]Includes summer full-time or other full-time employment of more than three months duration.
[b]Higher scores suggest a more external perception of control.
[c]Higher scores suggest increased anxiety.
[d]All employment applications ratings were made on a 10-point scale, with 10 as the highest point.
[e]All ratings were divided by interview duration.

Employment Applications. Personnel specialists gave application forms overall means ranging from 3.125 to 6.938 for the five rated attributes. Analyses (X^2) revealed no differences on any attributes for age or previous work experience.

Job Interview. Controlling for length, ratings were divided by interview duration. Means represent ratio scores for eight variables of interest. There were no significant differences (X^2) on any variables subdivided by age or previous work history.

Training

Based on assessment findings and on allocations of continuation program resources, personnel, and time, two areas were identified as having high likelihood for improvement through brief, intensive training: completing an employment application form neatly, thoroughly, and appropriately for each item of requested information; and responding in a job interview using positive and facilitative responses of eye contact and smiles, answering all questions, and giving positive and specific information about life experiences and personal background. Previous research validates these skills as necessary for successful job interviewing.[21]

An interventive program was designed in which one half of the participants were assigned randomly to a training condition, with remaining participants assigned to a control condition. Young women in the control condition received only pretest and posttest batteries. Training-condition participants were involved in four 90-minute, weekly group sessions, following a paradigm similar to ones used in other skills-acquisition investigations.[22] Each group session began with a description of one or two desirable skills. Leaders demonstrated these skills, and group members role played and practiced them in pairs. Rotating among participants, leaders gave feedback, reinforcement, and instructions. Sessions also included instruction and practice in completing employment applications. Young women learned to read applications carefully and to give written presentations of themselves, clearly specifying positive attributes and experience.

Evaluation

All participants completed a posttest battery identical to the pretest battery given earlier. Comparing pretest to posttest change scores between the two conditions quantified differences attributable to training. Results of these comparisons on Locus-of-Control Scales, Affect Adjective Check Lists, and the five employment application ratings are summarized in figure 9-1. Results showed consistently more positive changes for training-condition participants than for control-condition participants. Young women receiving training showed reduced externality on Locus of Control and were less anxious as measured by Affect Adjective Check List. Personnel specialists rated employment applications written by trained young women as neater, showing more competence, more relevant academic qualifications, and better employment histories than those of participants not trained. Of special note is the category "recommend hiring/placement": ratings by personnel specialists showed mean change scores nearly 10 times greater for training-condition participants than for control-condition participants.

Change-score means for both conditions on job-interview ratings, depicted in figure 9-2, confirm other findings and revealed greater gains for trained participants than for those in the control condition. Trained participants had more desirable changes in eye contact, smiles, and positive self-

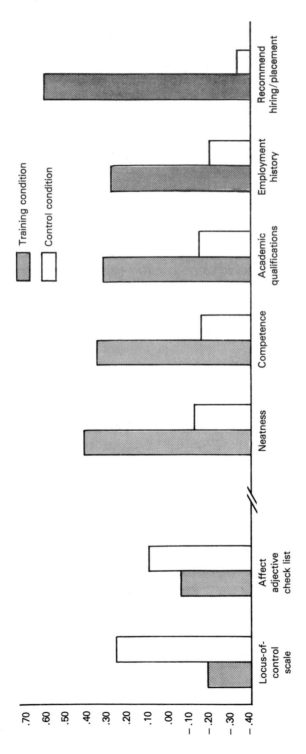

[a]Higher scores on locus of control indicate a more external perception of control, while higher scores on the affect-adjective check list indicate increased anxiety. All other ratings are on a 10-point scale, with 10 as the highest point.

Figure 9-1. Pretest to Posttest Change-Score Means for Training-Condition Participants and Control-Condition Participants on Locus-of-Control Scale, Affect-Adjective Check List, and Employment-Application Ratings[a]

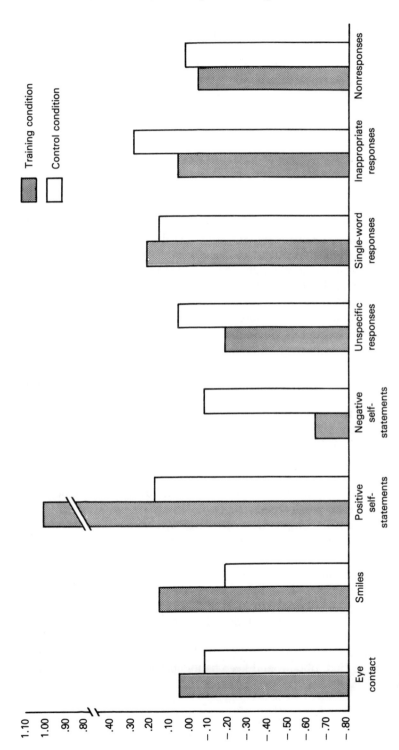

^aAll ratings were divided by interview duration.

Figure 9-2. Pretest to Posttest Change-Score Means for Training-Condition Participants and Control-Condition Participants on Job-Interview Ratings[a]

statements than had control participants. These participants, compared to those in the control condition, decreased pre- to posttest frequency of negative self-statements, unspecific responses, inappropriate responses, and nonresponses. Single-word responses is the only variable on which trained young women showed negative pre- to posttest movement: They had a higher mean change score than had control participants.

Discussion

This study examined variables relevant to improving teenage mothers' ability to apply for jobs successfully—a crucial first step toward economic self-sufficiency. Assessment battery data revealed study participants not differing from available norms on measures of self-esteem and performance anxiety nor on any variable when subdivided by age and previous work experience. Examination of pretest data identified a group of employment-application skill deficits. Intervention was implemented to help young women acquire these skills. Trained participants perceived themselves as more in control and less anxious than did those not trained. Based on written employment applications, training-condition participants were more likely to be recommended for hiring: further, videotaped performances showed these women more competent in a job-interview situation.

Promising study findings have implications for others seeking to quantify and change aspects of large-scale social and economic problems. Evolving out of concern for increasing the economic self-sufficiency of teenage mothers, study strategy identified quantifiable targets for direct assessment, intervention, and evaluation. Economic self-sufficiency results from employment; employment requires being hired; being hired depends, in part, on competent job-interview skills. For study purposes, job-interview skills were defined as completing written employment applications and performing well in personal interviews. Such a level of specificity permitted assessment, focused training, and subsequent evaluation grounded in observable and quantifiable behavior.

Future research should build on and expand present work. Two unexplored areas are identifying skills needed to locate jobs and skills necessary to keep them once applicants complete the interview process and are hired. This study represents one positive, data-based departure point for those interested in assisting teenage mothers and other chronically unemployed populations to find, obtain, and keep badly needed jobs and thus improve their economic self-sufficiency.

Notes

1. W.H. Baldwin, "Adolescent Pregnancy and Childbearing—Growing Concerns for Americans," *Population Bulletin* 31 (2) (1976):1-36; W.B. Hunt II, "Adolescent Fertility: Risks and Consequences," *Population Reports* J (1976):157-175; National Center for Health Statistics, U.S. Department of Health, Education, and Welfare, "Teenage Childbearing: United States, 1966-75," *Monthly Vital Statistics Report* 16 (5) (1977):1-15.

2. F.F. Furstenberg, Jr., *Unplanned Parenthood: The Social Consequences of Teenage Childbearing* (New York: Free Press, 1976); A.P. Jurich and J.A..Jurich, "The Lost Adolescence Syndrome," *Family Coordinator* 24 (1975):357-361; J.A. Menken, "The Health and Social Consequences of Teenage Childbearing," *Family Planning Perspectives* 4 (1972):45-53.

3. R.E. Helfer, and C.H. Kempe, "The Child's Need for Early Recognition, Immediate Care and Protection," in *Helping the Battered Child and His Family*, ed. C.H. Kempe and R.E. Helfer, (Philadelphia: J.B. Lippincott, 1972); Hoffman, cited in U.S. Senate, *Report to Accompany S. 2910, Adolescent Health, Services, and Pregnancy Prevention and Care Act of 1978* (95th Cong., 2nd sess., Calendar No. 1129, August 16, 1978) (Washington, D.C.: Government Printing Office, 1978).

4. Jurich and Jurich, "The Lost Adolescence Syndrome"; C.A. Nettleton and D.W. Cline, "Dating Patterns, Sexual Relationships and Use of Contraceptives of 700 Unwed Mothers During a Two-year Period Following Delivery," *Adolescence* 10 (1975):45-47.

5. I.W. Gabrielson, L.V. Klerman, J.B. Currie, N.C. Tyler, and J.F. Jekel, "Suicide Attempts in a Population Pregnant as Teenagers," *American Journal of Public Health* 60 (1970):2289-2301.

6. Alan Guttmacher Institute, *11 Million Teenagers: What Can be Done about the Epidemic of Adolescent Pregnancies in the United States* (New York: Planned Parenthood Federation of America, 1976); K.A. Moore and L.H. Waite, "Early Childbearing and Educational Attainment," *Family Planning Perspectives* 9 (1977):220-225.

7. Bureau of Labor Statistics, U.S. Department of Labor, *Employment and Earnings: February 1978* (Washington, D.C.: Government Printing Office, 1978); H.B. Presser, *Social Consequences of Teenage Childbearing*, paper presented at the Conference on the Consequences of Adolescent Pregnancy and Childbearing, Bethesda, Maryland, October 1975.

8. J.J. Card and L.L. Wise, "Teenage Mothers and Teenage Fathers: The Impact of Early Childbearing on the Parents' Personal and Professional Lives," *Family Planning Perspectives* 10 (1978):199-205.

9. L. Bacon, "Early Motherhood, Accelerated Role Transition, and Social Pathologies," *Social Forces* 52 (1974):333-341.

10. Presser, *Social Consequences of Teenage Childbearing*.

11. Ibid.

12. K.A. Moore, "Teenage Childbirth and Welfare Dependency," *Family Planning Perspectives* 10 (1978):233-235.

13. M. Zelnik and J.K. Kantner, "First Pregnancies to Women Aged 15-19: 1976 and 1971," *Family Planning Perspectives* 48 (1978):663-672.

14. S.P. Schinke, "A School-based Model for Teenage Pregnancy Prevention," *Social Work in Education*, in press; S.P. Schinke, "Health and Social Needs Accompanying Adolescent Childbearing: Research and Implications for Practice," in *Meeting the Health and Social Needs of the Adolescent*, ed. W.H. Hall and C.Y. Young (Pittsburgh: University of Pittsburgh Graduate School of Public Health, in press); S.P. Schinke and L.D. Gilchrist, "Adolescent Pregnancy: An Interpersonal Skill Training Approach to Prevention," *Social Work in Health Care* 3 (1977):159-167; S.P. Schinke, L.D. Gilchrist, and R.W. Small, "Preventing Unwanted Adolescent Pregnancy: A Cognitive-Behavioral Approach," *American Journal of Orthopsychiatry* 49 (1979):81-88; S.P. Schinke, L.D. Gilchrist, T.E. Smith, and S.E. Wong, "Improving Teenage Mothers' Ability to Compete for Jobs," *Social Work Research and Abstracts* 14 (3) (1978):25-29.

15. J.R. Barbee and E.C. Keil, "Experimental Techniques of Job Interview Training for the Disadvantaged: Videotape Feedback, Behavior Modification, and Microcounseling," *Journal of Applied Psychology* 58 (1973):209-213; E.C. Keil and J.R. Barbee, "Behavior Modification and Training the Disadvantaged Job Interviewee," *Vocational Guidance Quarterly* 22 (1973):50-56; C.D. Miller and G. Oetting, "Barriers to Employment and the Disadvantaged," *The Personnel and Guidance Journal* 56 (1977):89-93; C.M. Mills and T.L. Walter, "A Behavioral Employment Intervention Program for Reducing Juvenile Delinquency," *Behavior Therapy* 8 (1977):270-272.

16. S. Nowicki, Jr., and B.R. Strickland, "A Locus of Control Scale for Children," *Journal of Consulting and Clinical Psychology* 40 (1973):148-154.

17. Barbee and Keil, "Experimental Techniques," p. 209.

18. M. Zuckerman and B. Lubin, *Manual for the Multiple Affect Adjective Check List* (San Diego: Educational and Industrial Testing Service, 1965).

19. Nowicki and Strickland, "A Locus of Control Scale for Children."

20. Zuckerman and Lubin, *Manual*.

21. M.R. Clowers and R.T. Fraser, "Employment Interview Literature: A Perspective for the Counselor," *The Vocational Guidance Quarterly* 26

(1977):13-26; W. Stevens and L. Tornatzky, "The Effects of a Job-interview Skills Workshop on Drug-abuse Clients," *Journal of Employment Counseling* 13 (1976):156-163.

22. Schinke and Gilchrist, "Adolescent Pregnancy"; Schinke, Gilchrist, and Small, "Preventing Unwanted Adolescent Pregnancy"; S.P. Schinke, L.D. Gilchrist, T.E. Smith, and S.E. Wong, "Group Interpersonal Skills Training in a Natural Setting: An Experimental Study," *Behavioral Research and Therapy* 17 (1979):149-154; S.P. Schinke and S.D. Rose, "Interpersonal Skill Training in Groups," *Journal of Counseling Psychology* 23 (1976):442-448; S.P. Schinke and S.D. Rose, "Assertive Training in Groups," in *Group Therapy: A Behavioral Approach*, ed. S.D. Rose (Englewood Cliffs, N.J.: Prentice-Hall, 1977); S.P. Schinke, T.E. Smith, L.D. Gilchrist, and S.E. Wong, "Interviewing Skills Training: An Empirical Investigation," *Journal of Social Service Research* 1 (1978):391-401.

10 Marrying, Divorcing, Living Together, and Working: Effects of Changing American Family Structure on the Popularity of Social Security

Yung-Ping Chen

Social security has been losing popularity in recent years. We suggest that one of the reasons is the inhospitable environment for social security that has been created by changes in the family structure during the last quarter century. Because social security is a valuable economic-security mechanism to families, changes in the structure of families affect the financial outcome of social security and therefore the acceptance of the program.

This chapter is divided into four main parts. First, we discuss the meaning of social security to American families, now and in the future, in terms of the distribution of beneficiaries by their status as insured workers, or as dependents and survivors (spouses, children, and parents) of insured workers. Next we point out the changes in family relationships and work role of women during the last two decades or so. Third, we speculate on the effect of the growing phenomenon of "singlehood" (never married, separated, and divorced persons) on the acceptance of social security. Fourth, we briefly analyze criticisms of the social-security protection in relation to married women and proposed ideas for reform.

Meaning of Social Security to American Families

Social security is not only an income-replacement program for the retired workers who are covered, it also is a source of income for eligible disabled

Discussed here is only one of the factors for the reduced support for social security. Other factors are higher social security taxes, changing age composition, and changing income distribution. Social security refers to the cash-benefit portion of the Old-age, Survivors, Disability, and Health Insurance Program (OASDI). For discussions of actuarial data, the author is grateful to Harry J. Kingerski and Orlo R. Nichols, both of the Office of the Actuary, Social Security Administration, although neither they nor the Office of the Actuary should be implicated in this writing venture. He also gratefully acknowledges helpful comments by Robert J. Myers, Paul C. Glick, Elizabeth Waldman, Sylvia Lane, and Kay Powell, which led to substantive and expositional clarity. Parts of the material are expanded from passages in Yung-Ping Chen, *Social Security in a Changing Society: An Introduction to Programs, Concepts, and Issues* (Bryn Mawr, Penn.: McCahan Foundation for Research in Economic Security, 1980).

workers. As such, social security means much to these workers' families, for the benefits provide some measure of economic security to them. But social security means more to these families than just payments to the retired or disabled worker, because cash benefits are also payable to eligible *dependents and survivors* of retired and disabled workers. Table 10-1 enumerates the categories of beneficiaries according to their status as workers or as dependents and survivors.

About 62 percent of the 35 million beneficiaries at the end of 1979 were retired and disabled workers. The remainder, 38 percent (or 13¼ million persons), were spouses, children, and parents of insured workers. Spouses (as dependents or survivors) comprised 24 percent of all the beneficiaries, and children accounted for nearly 14 percent. Parents represented a negligible percentage.

Although social security is a basic retirement-income program, only slightly more than half the beneficiaries were retired workers. Social security is therefore an important economic-security measure for workers and their families because of the financial protection it provides even before retirement.

The distribution of beneficiaries is projected to change in the future, as shown in table 10-2.[1] First, it is estimated that a greater proportion of OASDI benefits would be received by retired workers: Whereas in 1979 only

Table 10-1
Distribution of OASDI Beneficiaries by Type of Recipients, December 1979

		Persons	*Percent*
I.	Insured workers		
	A. Retired	19.0 million	54.1%
	B. Disabled	2.9	8.3
	(subtotal of A and B)	(21.9)	(62.4)
II.	Dependents and survivors of insured workers		
	A. Spouses		
	1. Of deceased workers	4.9	14.0
	2. Of retired workers	3.0	8.5
	3. Of disabled workers	.5	1.4
	(subtotal of 1 to 3)	(8.4)	(23.9)
	B. Children and parents		
	1. Children of deceased workers	2.7	7.7
	2. Children of retired workers	.7	2.0
	3. Children of disabled workers	1.4	4.0
	4. Parents of deceased workers	.02	—
	(subtotal of 1 to 4)	(4.8)	(13.7)
III.	Total of I and II	35.1 million	100.0%

Source: Social Security Administration.

Table 10-2
Distribution of OASDI Beneficiaries, by Type of Recipients in Selected Years, 1979-2050
(percent; number of persons in thousands in parentheses)

Year[a]	Retired Workers	Disabled Workers	Spouses (dependents and survivors)	Children (dependents and survivors)	Total[b]
1979	54.2	8.2	23.9	13.7	100.0
	(18,970)	(2,870)	(8,362)	(4,794)	(35,013)
1990	59.7	9.2	21.2	9.9	100.0
	(25,106)	(3,862)	(8,909)	(4,147)	(42,031)
2000	60.2	11.1	19.0	9.6	100.0
	(28,136)	(5,209)	(8,879)	(4,496)	(46,727)
2020	67.4	10.9	13.5	8.2	100.0
	(45,035)	(7,260)	(9,042)	(5,447)	(66,791)
2050	72.8	9.2	11.1	7.0	100.0
	(58,120)	(7,316)	(8,844)	(5,575)	(79,862)

Source: Data from Social Security Administration; 1979 figures are actual experience as of December. Later years' are as of June.

Notes:

[a]Figures for 1990 and beyond are based on the Alternative II estimates, as explained in footnote 1.

[b]Includes a small number of aged parents (17,000 in 1979 and 7,000 in 1990 and later years). Does not include "special age-72 beneficiaries," of whom there were 112,000 in 1979, but there will be very few in 1990 and beyond.

54.2 percent of the beneficiaries were retired workers, that percentage would rise to about 60 percent in 1990-2000, to 67.4 percent in 2020, and to nearly 73 percent in 2050.

Second, spouses in 1979 accounted for 24 percent of all beneficiaries. That percentage is projected to decline to about 20 percent in 1990-2000, to 13.5 percent in 2020, and to only 11.1 percent in 2050.

Third, the proportion of beneficiaries who are children will decline from about 14 percent in 1979 to approximately 10 percent in 1990-2000, to 8 percent in 2020, and to a mere 7 percent in 2050.

The projected increase in spouse and children beneficiaries is considerably less than that in retired and disabled-worker beneficiaries. There were nearly 8.4 million spouses who received benefits in 1979, and that number would rise to slightly over 8.8 million in 2050, representing a mere 5.8 percent increase over the next seven decades (1979-2050). 4.8 million children were beneficiaries in 1979, and the count would be 5.6 million in 2050, representing a growth of about 16 percent during 1979-2050. By contrast between 1979 and 2050 the number of retired workers as beneficiaries would rise more than threefold, from about 19 million in 1979 to some 58 million in 2050, and the roll of disabled workers is expected to increase by two and a half times to 7.3 million in 2050.

The projected changes in the OASDI beneficiary categories reflect changing social, demographic, and economic trends concerning marriage, divorce, living arrangements, and labor-force behavior, as well as fertility and mortality. These changes affect family structure and age composition in the society.

Changes in Family Relationships, Lifestyles, and Workstyles

Changes in marriage and the family, living arrangements, and labor force behavior during the last two decades or so may be captured from a brief recitation of some statistics.[2]

Delay in First Marriage

In 1956 the median ages at first marriage were 22.5 years for men and 20.1 years for women. Some twenty years later, in 1977, the median ages at first marriage were 24.0 years for men and 21.6 years for women. A delay of about one and one half years took place in the period, 1956-1977. Delay in marriage was especially great among women in their early twenties. The proportion of women who had never married at ages 20 to 24 was 28 percent in 1960; it increased by more than one half to 45 percent in 1977. During the same period, 1960-1977, the proportion of women in their late twenties who were still single rose from 10.5 percent to 16.1 percent.

Average Family Size

During the early 1900s the average family had four children; during the 1930s, three children; during the 1950s, three and one half children; during the 1960s, two and one half children. From 1965 to 1976, the birthrate per 1,000 population declined by 24 percent—from 19.4 to 14.7. This rate seems to have stabilized at the 15.0 level in the last several years. The average number of children born per woman will probably remain at 2.1 children, according to most observers.

Divorce, Remarriage, and Separation

The divorce rate increased dramatically in the last two decades. From 1960 to 1979, the divorce rate more than doubled, from 2.2 to 5.3 per 1,000 population. The remarriage rate has moved down in recent years; from 1972 to 1975, the rate declined by 17 percent. Even the remarriage rate after widowhood went down during the same period of time—2.5 percent less in 1975 than in 1972.

Separation has become more prevalent as well. In 1976 the number of separated persons was about half as large as the number of divorced persons, 3.8 million as compared to 7.2 million. In 1976, 3 percent of the men at ages 40 to 44 reported that they were separated, and 6 percent reported that they were divorced; the corresponding proportions for women at ages 35-39 were 5 percent separated and 9 percent divorced.

Time Spent in and out of Marriage

People are in the marital state for fewer years these days. Divorces took place sooner in 1975 than in 1967. In 1967 half of the divorces after first marriage occurred during the first 8 years after marriage, and half of the redivorces after remarriages happened during the first 6 years. In 1975 the corresponding number was close to 7 years for the divorces after first marriage and about 5 years for the redivorces. In other words, divorces after first marriages are now happening about six months to a year sooner than was the case 10 years ago, and redivorces are taking place about a year and one half sooner.

Living Together without Being Married

Unmarried couples of opposite sex living together have increased substantially in recent years. In 1979 about 2.7 million adults were sharing their living quarters with only one other unmarried adult, an increase of 40 percent in two years from about 1.9 million in 1977. The corresponding number in 1970 was 1 million. Between 1970 and 1979 the growth of this type of household was nearly 8 times for those 25 to 44 years of age, and about 9.5 times for those under age 25. Among those age 45 and over there was practically no increase during the decade, and among those 65 and over a slight decline occurred.[3] While there are no firm statistics on couples of the same sex living together, this lifestyle is becoming more widely recognized.

Single-Parent Families

Families maintained by a woman without the presence of a husband comprised 13 percent of all families in 1975, up from 11 percent in 1970. In both years only 2 or 3 percent of families were maintained by a man without a wife present. From 1970 to 1975, married-couple families increased by only 6 percent, but single-parent families went up by 30 percent. In 1975 more than 60 percent of the single-parent families headed by women had one or more children living with them.

Working Women

The most significant impact of the social and demographic changes just cited has been on women. Changes in family structure and labor-force behavior of women are interactive.

During the 1970s a record number of women entered or reentered the paid labor force. From 1971 to 1978, an average of more than 1 million women joined the labor force each year, with 1.9 million in 1978. By the first half of 1979 over 43 million women were in the labor force. They represented 41 percent of all paid workers, and 51 percent of all women over the age of 15. Between 1970 and 1978 the labor-force participation rate by women at ages 25 to 34 increased from 45 percent to 62 percent—an increase of nearly 38 percent. More than 70 percent of women in the 25-34 age group were married and living with their husbands and had children under age 18. The labor-force participation rate for all women with preschool age children was 30 percent in 1970 but jumped to 44 percent in 1978, an increase of nearly 47 percent.

The number of all women in the labor force who are separated or divorced increased from 3.3 million in March 1970 to 5.7 million in March 1978, an increase of about 73 percent in 8 years.

In summary, the social, demographic, and economic environment has undergone great changes in the last few decades. When social security first started making monthly payments in 1940, the traditional family unit consisted of a wage-earning husband, a homemaking dependent wife, and children. Most marriages lasted a lifetime. Only 17 percent of married women worked for pay. Today the typical family can no longer be characterized simply by a working husband with a dependent wife and children. In 1978 58 percent (or more than 27 million) of the married-couple families had two or more earners. Separation and divorce, living together, and single parenthood have become more prevalent. And women have entered the paid labor force in record numbers, with 47 percent of married women now in the labor force.

The Singlehood Phenomenon and the "Money's Worth" of Social Security

Because of the various changes in the family structure, social security tends to be less valuable or perceived to be less valuable to an increasing number of persons who are in either a singlehood state (never married, separated, divorced, or cohabiting) or a singlehood mind (contemplating separation or divorce). One way to illustrate this tendency is to consider the question of "money's worth" of social security.

The money's worth question basically refers to the relationship between the benefits to be gained and the taxes to be paid by covered workers under social security. The payroll tax rate (applied on wages and salaries up to the taxable ceiling) is uniform for all covered workers, with a separate uniform tax rate for all self-employed persons. Single men and single women pay the same tax rate as do married persons. Married persons with dependents and those without dependents also pay the same tax rate. Taxes among persons vary only as their earnings do (up to the maximum taxable ceiling). If earnings from employment are the same, workers pay the same taxes, but are entitled to different amounts of benefits. Moreover, a working wife who pays social-security taxes just like other workers, may not receive two types of benefits—her own retirement benefit as well as the wife's benefit.[4]

Over the years there have been differences in financial payout under social security: between single persons and married persons, between married persons with children and those without, and between married couples with wives working and those without. Such differences were not important when the great majority of adults had a lifetime marriage with children and most married women were not in the labor force or were not in paid work as a career. However, in a world in which singlehood is becoming the lifestyle of increasingly large numbers of persons, this problem has become more prominent. In addition, since so many women have joined the labor force, differences in social-security payout have taken on new significance.

Concerning the money's worth question, table 10-3 helps to illustrate the differences in payout between three hypothetical workers with median earnings who became covered by social security in 1978 at age 22. The benefit-tax ratio is used to suggest the value of social security to a worker. Such a ratio is obtained by dividing "the OASDI benefits to be gained" by "the employee taxes to be paid," both in present-value terms.[5]

The benefit-tax ratio is estimated to be 1.41 for the unmarried male worker (or the married male worker whose wife works in the paid labor force and has a larger benefit from her own work record than from her husband's), 3.20 for the married male worker (with a wife who does not work in the paid labor force), and 1.90 for the unmarried female worker (or the married female worker whose husband has a larger benefit from his own record than from hers). Since a large benefit-tax ratio means a greater financial payout, the married male worker fares the best, and the unmarried male worker fares the worst. The reason that the unmarried female worker fares better than does the unmarried male worker is that the life expectancy is longer for women. Because of the family status the married male worker may expect the greatest financial payout.

Table 10-3
Workers with Median Earnings Becoming Covered in 1978 at Age 22: Components of Present Values of Benefits and Taxes

I. Unmarried male worker		
A. Benefits to be gained		
1. Old age	$20,856	
2. Disability	6,648	
3. Total benefits to be gained		$27,504
B. Worker's OASDI taxes to be paid		19,557
C. Benefit-tax ratio		1.41
II. Married male worker		
A. Benefits to be gained		
1. Old age (to worker)	$20,856	
2. Disability (to worker)	6,648	
3. Old age (to spouse and surviving spouse)	25,084	
4. Disability (to spouse and surviving spouse)	1,313	
5. Death before retirement	8,708	
6. Total benefits to be gained		$62,609
B. Worker's OASDI taxes to be paid		19,557
C. Benefit-tax ratio		3.20
III. Unmarried female worker		
A. Benefits to be gained		
1. Old age	$32,187	
2. Disability	6,713	
3. Total benefits to be gained		$38,900
B. Worker's OASDI taxes to be paid		20,421
C. Benefit-tax ratio		1.90

Source: Taken and reconstructed from "Some Comparisons of the Value of a Worker's Social Security Taxes and Benefits," *Actuarial Note* Number 95, April 1978, table 3. (Social Security Administration, U.S. Department of Health, Education, and Welfare.)

It is suggested that the singlehood phenomenon has created a measure of dissatisfaction with social security. Single persons (never married men and women) might feel that they are not getting their money's worth because married persons are garnering high payouts under social security. They might feel this way even if they may later marry. Divorced men might feel disenchanted with social security for the same reason, even if remarriage may ensue. They might even feel that the taxes they paid while married were wasted, even though their ex-wives may be eligible for benefits. Separated men might be in a like mind, even though marital reconciliation may occur or, in case of eventual divorce, their ex-wives may be eligible for benefits. With single persons (never married men and women, separated and divorced men) in the labor force numbering more than 28.4 million in March 1978, the potential discontent with social security may be widespread.[6] This total was larger than the total of 18.6 million in March 1970, an increase of 9.8 million or 53 percent in 8 years. Seen in this light, the lessening of popular support for social security in the last decade or so may be more understandable.

It should be emphasized that the benefit-tax ratios cited were computed for hypothetical workers who are assumed to be continuously employed, have covered earnings that rise steadily, and do not change their marital status. Nonetheless, these ratios may be used to suggest the reasons for the concern of single persons about the value of social security to them. The longer a person is in a singlehood state or the more a person is in a singlehood frame of mind, the more doubt or questioning there will be about the money's worth of social security.

Married Women and the Social-Security Protection[7]

With the increasing participation of married women in the labor force, there have arisen many criticisms of social security in terms of how they fare under it. Alleged charges of unfair or inadequate treatment of married women by social security may be described or dramatized as consisting of these types of penalties: (1) penalty for working; (2) penalty for divorce; (3) penalty for widowhood; and (4) penalty for homemaking and/or childrearing.

Penalty for working refers to these problems: (a) Since a nonworking or homemaking married woman would receive a wife's benefit based on her husband's earnings credits, a working wife may feel that she is no better off for the taxes she pays into social security; (b) a man and wife who both work (a two-earner couple) receive less in benefits than a couple with only one spouse working when total earnings of the two couples are identical; and (c) the surviving spouse of a two-earner couple gets less in benefits than does the surviving spouse of a one-earner couple when total earnings of the two couples are identical.

Penalty for divorce refers to these problems: (a) A divorced wife or a surviving divorced wife has no social-security protection based on her ex-husband's earnings credits unless their marriage lasted for at least 10 years; and (b) a divorced wife does not receive benefits until her ex-husband retires, becomes disabled, or dies.

Penalty for widowhood refers to the problem that no benefits are payable to a widow under age 60 unless she is either at least age 50 and disabled or is caring for a child or children of her deceased husband.

Penalty for homemaking and/or childrearing refers to these problems: (a) A nonworking or homemaking married woman is not insured against disability, and her survivors are not entitled to benefits when she dies; (b) when a woman takes time out from paid work to raise a family, she loses disability income protection if she does not meet the "recent-work" requirement (20 quarters of coverage in the 40-quarter period ending with the quarter in which disability occurs, with fewer required quarters of coverage for persons under age 31); and (c) when a woman takes time out from paid work to raise a family her working career is shortened, her lifetime average-earnings credits are reduced because of many zero-earnings years, and as a result her retirement benefits are smaller than if she had not had children.

While none of the problems cited are the intended results of deliberate policy of social security and several of those problems have been created by circumstances external to social security, treatment of women has been an important issue confronting the nation's basic program of income support in the event of old age, disability, or death. In recent years several government bodies have been engaged in extensive studies of this issue. The following is a brief reference to such recent efforts.

In February 1979 a Department of Health, Education, and Welfare task force made public the results of a study mandated by Congress in 1977. Without endorsing either plan, the task force suggested two models for comprehensive change in the treatment of women: an "earnings-sharing" approach and a "two-tier benefit" approach. Under the earnings-sharing approach a worker's social-security benefits would be based on his or her earnings when single, and on one half the combined earnings of a couple when married. At divorce each spouse's wage record would be credited with half the couple's combined earnings during the marriage, regardless of the length of the marriage. Therefore each spouse would get a social-security retirement benefit in his or her own right.

Under the two-tier approach the existing benefit structure would be replaced. The new plan would provide a "flat-rate benefit" (as the first tier) to every U.S. resident who meets the age requirements or who is disabled, regardless of earnings; then it would provide an "earnings-related benefit" (as a second tier) that would be based on earnings credits under social security. The total benefit for an aged or disabled person would be the sum of these two benefits. The second-tier benefit structure employs the earnings-sharing approach. Thus at divorce each spouse's wage record would be credited with one half the couple's combined earnings while married; and when one spouse dies, the surviving spouse would inherit all the earnings credits of the deceased spouse.

While the above models appear simple, the implementation of either would entail complex changes in the present social-security program. In December 1979 the 1979 Advisory Council on Social Security announced in its report that the majority of its members found the sharing of earnings between spouses to be the most promising approach and recommended more studies and debate. Furthermore, by a narrow majority the council recommended that Congress consider immediate implementation of two changes: (1) Earnings-sharing at divorce, which would permit persons divorced after at least 10 years of marriage to receive retirement benefits based on shared earnings; and (2) earnings-inheriting at spouse's death, which would permit aged widows or widowers to receive benefits on the basis of the couple's combined earnings credits. These changes would, according to the council, address the needs of divorced women and of elderly widows and widowers.

There is no indication at this time whether the preceding changes would be mandated by Congress. Moreover, other issues affecting women under social security await early solution. The longer it takes to resolve the various problems affecting women in general and two-earner families in particular, the longer the feeling of dissatisfaction with social security on the part of a significant number of individuals will persist. Meanwhile, it appears important to call attention to the fact that under the existing system working wives are earning valuable credits toward disability benefits (in case of permanent and total disability), survivors benefits (in case of her death with eligible survivors), and retirement benefits (in case of her retiring earlier than her husband).

Since earnings of women are lower than those of men, the working woman will receive a larger amount from a wife's benefit than from a retirement benefit based on her own earnings. (The differentials in median earnings between men and women both as year-round, full-time workers have been around 60 percent for years: 58 percent in 1939 and 60-61 percent in May 1978). Because a working married woman can only receive the larger of two types of benefits, it might easily be concluded that she has paid social-security taxes in vain. However, the working woman is earning credits toward valuable income protection.

As more women work they will be acquiring credits toward social-security retirement benefits based on their own earnings. Table 10-4 shows the distribution of persons receiving old-age benefits derived from their own work records, as estimated by the Social Security Administration. Whereas in 1980 women accounted for some 46 percent of all old-age beneficiaries, that proportion is estimated to reach 56 percent in 2050. Women would make up more than half of retirement beneficiaries in just two decades, in the year 2000. In absolute numbers, woman recipients would increase by 5.3 million in 20 years, from 8.9 million in 1979 to 14.2 million in 2000. The longer term growth is even more dramatic, as the figures in table 10-4 show.

In addition to retirement benefits, they also would be eligible for disability benefits. Table 10-5 shows the distribution of disability benefits between male and female workers in selected years, 1958-2050. The proportion of disability beneficiaries represented by women workers has increased in the past and is expected to grow in the future. When such benefits were first paid in 1958, only one in five beneficiaries was a woman worker. Twenty years later, in 1978, almost one of every three beneficiaries was a woman. This proportion is projected to rise to 35 percent in 1990, 38 percent in 2000, and 41 percent in 2020-2050.

Table 10-4
Distribution of Old-Age Retirement-Benefit Recipients by Men and Women Workers in Selected Years, 1980-2050
(percent; number of persons in millions in parentheses)

Year	Men	Women
1980	53.6	46.4
	(10.3)	(8.9)
1990	51.0	49.0
	(12.8)	(12.3)
2000	49.5	50.5
	(13.9)	(14.2)
2020	46.4	53.6
	(20.9)	(24.1)
2050	43.7	56.3
	(25.4)	(32.7)

Source: Unpublished data provided by the Office of the Actuary, Social Security Administration.

In absolute numbers women workers as disability beneficiaries registered a near twentyfold growth in 20 years between 1958 and 1978, whereas disabled-men beneficiaries increased some elevenfold, a considerably smaller rate. The growth rate from 1978 to 2050 is projected to triple for women and double for men. Thus increasing numbers of women workers would be receiving disability benefits. This is an important protection.

Concluding Remarks

The purpose of this chapter is a simple one, to explain one of the causes of the lessened support for social security in recent years: certain changes affecting the traditional family as a key institution in society. New living arrangements among men and women and the shifting labor-force behavior of women have raised questions about the financial payout to, and fairness of treatment of, various groups of persons for whom social security was designed to provide protection. Confidence in social security will not be restored unless the system is modified to adapt to new social and economic environments, including problems caused by the changing family and work relationships.

Table 10-5
Distribution of Disability-Benefit Recipients by Men and Women Workers in Selected Years, 1958-2050
(percent; number of persons in thousands in parentheses)

Year	Men	Women
1958	78.6 (176)	21.4 (48)
1960	73.1 (261)	26.9 (96)
1970	64.5 (680)	35.5 (374)
1978	67.7 (1,966)	32.3 (939)
1990	65.2 (2,517)	34.8 (1,345)
2000	61.9 (3,223)	38.1 (1,986)
2020	58.6 (4,257)	41.4 (3,003)
2050	58.7 (4,294)	41.3 (3,022)

Source: Unpublished data provided by the Office of the Actuary, Social Security Administration.

Notes

1. Cost estimates (and therefore estimates of numbers of beneficiaries) are affected by a number of economic and demographic factors such as rates of fertility, mortality, net immigration, labor-force participation, employment and unemployment, productivity and economic growth, inflation, retirement, disability, and the like. The low-cost estimate refers to the net effect of the developments in the preceding factors that result in a low cost for the program. The high-cost estimate is just the opposite. The intermediate-cost estimate lies between the low- and high-cost estimates. Alternative II is the intermediate-cost estimate.

2. Statistical information in this section is collected from Paul C. Glick, "The Future of the American Family," *Current Population Reports*, Special Studies, Series P-23, no. 78, U.S. Bureau of the Census, January 1979; Paul C. Glick and Arthur J. Norton, "Marrying, Divorcing, and Living-together in the United States Today," *Population Bulletin*, vol. 32, no. 5 (Population Reference Bureau, Washington, D.C., 1977); Janet L.

Norwood, "New Approaches to Statistics on the Family," *Monthly Labor Review*, July 1977, pp. 31-37; Janet L. Norwood and Elizabeth Waldman, "Women in the Labor Force: Some New Data Series," Report 575, U.S. Department of Labor, Bureau of Labor Statistics, 1979; National Center for Health Statistics, "Births, Marriages, Divorces, and Deaths for November 1979," *Monthly Vital Statistics Report*, Public Health Service, No. 80-1120, vol. 28, no. 11, February 8, 1980; and U.S. Bureau of the Census, "Marital Status and Living Arrangements: March 1979," *Current Population Reports*, Series P-20, no. 349, February 1980.

3. These data may simply be a count of unrelated persons of the opposite sex living in the same household as, for example, in cases where elderly widows are renting rooms to male students. Therefore, these statistics do not necessarily imply any marriage-like relationship between the persons involved. Interestingly, as the text points out, during the 1970s the greatest increase (very impressive gains) occurred among those under age 45. For older persons, there was either no increase or a slight decrease in this type of household. Census statistics on unmarried couples also contain separate counts for such couples with or without children present. In 1979, about 27 percent of unmarried couples (or 720,000 persons) were living together with one or more children in the same household. In reciting the above statistics we have not been concerned with whether or not these couples maintain a conjugal or sexual relationship. We are merely interested in pointing out the phenomenon of singlehood as it relates to social security.

4. Technically, the wife always gets her own benefit plus the excess, if any, of (1) wife's benefit over (2) own benefit. The rule of not allowing two types of benefits to be paid to a single beneficiary applies to "working husbands" as well; they cannot receive both their own benefit and a husband's or widower's benefit.

5. The meaning and function of the concept of present value may be explained as follows: The purpose of a benefit-tax ratio is to compare the magnitude of benefits with the magnitude of taxes. Both benefits and taxes are paid over a number of time periods, and they differ in amounts paid in each period. In order to compare these two series of dollar amounts, they must be converted into two single-sum payments. When a series of future payments is converted to a single-sum payment of today, the single sum is the "present value" of all payments to be made in the future. The single sum is the amount that, when invested beginning today at an assumed rate of interest, will produce enough funds to make future payments out of both principal and interest. Benefits (to be gained) and taxes (to be paid) must each be properly viewed as a series of future payments. Therefore, a single sum for the series of benefits and a single sum for the series of taxes may be computed as of a given date in order to compare them. In this instance, the present value of the benefits and the present value of the taxes are

computed as of the same date, January 1, 1978, at an assumed interest rate of 6.6 percent. In other words, the single sum of $27,504 shown in table 10-3, for the unmarried male worker is the amount that, if invested at 6.6 percent compound rate of interest from January 1, 1978, will produce sufficient funds (together with the principal) to pay the benefits over the period of time during which he is expected to receive these benefits. The single sum of $19,557, also shown in table 10-3, is the amount that, if invested at 6.6 percent from January 1, 1978 on, will generate enough funds (together with the original sum) to pay all the taxes due over the period of time being considered.

6. The total of 28.4 million persons was made up of 24 million never-married men and women, 1.7 million separated men, and 2.7 million divorced men. Separated and divorced women have not been included in the discussion because no OASDI benefits are payable to divorced husbands, divorced widowers, or disabled divorced widowers; nor are there benefits for widowed fathers or surviving divorced fathers who have one or more children in their care.

7. On issues of benefit inadequacies and unfair treatment of women, the following references contain detailed information: *Report of the HEW Task Force on the Treatment of Women under Social Security,* February 1978; Department of Health, Education, and Welfare, *Social Security and the Changing Role of Men and Women*, February 1979; and *Report of the 1979 Advisory Council on Social Security*, December 1979.

Index

Index

About the Contributors

Gordon E. Bivens is professor and head of the Department of Family Environment, Iowa State University. He received the B.S., M.S., and Ph.D. degrees from Iowa State. Dr. Bivens's interests include consumer economics, family economics, and the economics of human-resource development. He has published widely in professional journals and is coauthor of *Consumer Choice: The Economics of Personal Living* (1977).

Richard K. Armey is chairman of the Economics Department at North Texas State University. He received the B.A. from Jamestown College, the M.A. from the University of North Dakota, and the Ph.D. from the University of Oklahoma. Dr. Armey has taught at the University of Montana, West Texas State University, Austin College, and North Texas State University. He is the author of *Price Theory: A Policy-Welfare Approach* (1977) and has published several monographs and articles in professional journals. His primary research area is price and welfare theory, with special emphasis on problems of income distribution.

Bruce A. Chadwick is chairman of the Department of Sociology, Brigham Young University. He received the B.A., M.A., and Ph.D. degrees from Washington University in St. Louis. His research interests include race and ethnic relations and the family, and he is coinvestigator of a study of social change in Middletown.

C. Bradford Chappell received the Ph.D. degree in sociology from Brigham Young University and worked on the research team for the study of social change in Middletown. Dr. Chappell is currently working on a master's degree in social work and family therapy at the University of Utah.

Robert G. Steadman is an associate professor in the Department of Textiles and Clothing at Colorado State University, where he teaches the economics of textile and apparel industries. He received the B.S. and Ph.D. degrees from the University of New South Wales. Most of his research and publications have been in the area of heat and moisture transfer of clothing.

Hyman Joseph teaches in the Department of Economics at the University of Iowa. He received the Ph.D. degree in economics from Northwestern University and has published articles in scholarly journals in the areas of urban transportation, investment in physical capital, health economics, international tourism, and the economic determinants of fertility. His current interests are in the areas of human capital and decision making in nonprofit institutions.

Lawrence Carter is currently assistant professor of sociology at the University of Oregon. He received the Ph.D. degree from the University of Oregon. Dr. Carter has taught at the University of the Pacific and served as staff associate to the Center for the Coordination of Research on Social Indicators of the Social Science Research Council. He is presently engaged in research on human fertility, internal migration, and social indicators.

John Bishop is currently project associate at the Institute for Research on Poverty, University of Wisconsin. He received the B.A. from Oberlin College and the M.A. and Ph.D. from the University of Michigan. Dr. Bishop's research interests include the impacts of unemployment on mental health and marital interaction and policy measures designed to reduce unemployment.

Jacqueline Kasun is professor of economics at Humboldt State University. She received the B.A. degree from the University of California at Berkeley and the Ph.D. from Columbia University. Dr. Kasun is the author of two books and numerous articles on economics and social issues. Her articles have appeared in such publications as *Public Interest, The Christian Science Monitor*, and *Current History*, as well as in professional journals.

Steven Paul Schinke, Ph.D. is associate professor of social work and director of social services in the Child Development and Mental Retardation Center, University of Washington. Dr. Schinke's clinical, teaching, and research activities include social work with children, youths, and families and most recently have focused on problems associated with unwanted pregnancy among adolescents. He is the author of *Behavioral Methods in Social Work* (forthcoming).

Lewayne Dorman Gilchrist, M.S.W. is a doctoral candidate in social welfare at the University of Washington. Her interests focus on prevention of social and health problems among children, adolescents, and families.

Thomas Edward Smith, M.S.W. is a doctoral candidate in social welfare at the University of Washington. He is engaged in research on preventing health, social, and behavioral disorders and has published in the area of evaluating training curricula for paraprofessionals.

Yung-Ping Chen is professor of economics at The American College and research director at the McCahan Foundation for Research in Economic Security, Bryn Mawr, Pennsylvania. Currently on leave from UCLA, he previously held a Brookings Research Professorship at the Brookings Institution. Dr. Chen was actively involved with the 1971 White House Conference on Aging, over a three-year period as a commissioned author, delegate, consultant, and member of the Post-Conference Board. He recently served as a member of the Consultant Panel of Actuaries and Economists of the 1979 Advisory Council on Social Security. Dr. Chen's teaching and research interests include public finance, government expenditures, and financing social security. A frequent contributor to scholarly journals and congressional hearings, his most recent publications include *Social Security in a Changing Society: An Introduction to Programs, Concepts, and Issues* (1980) and *Unlocking Home Equity for the Elderly* (with Ken Scholen, 1980).

About the Editor

Stephen J. Bahr is an associate professor of family relations and sociology and an affiliate of the Family and Demographic Research Institute at Brigham Young University. He received the B.S. and M.S. degrees from Brigham Young University and the Ph.D. degree from Washington State University. Dr. Bahr's recent research has focused on the economic antecedents and consequences of divorce and the policy implications. He has taught at the University of Texas at Austin and recently spent a year at the Bush Institute for Child and Family Policy at the University of North Carolina.